In 2006, Vince Papale shot to international stardom as the subject of the Disney hit movie *Invincible*, which told the story of his rise from teacher and bartender to 30-year-old Philadelphia Eagles rookie and eventual special teams captain. But his unprecedented rise wasn't just a fluke or lucky break. Far from it.

Papale, a Philadelphia legend who's often called "the real life Rocky," knows a few things about how to reach your true potential in the face of internal or external challenges. It's why he's a sought-after motivational speaker all over the world and an inspiration to adults and children alike. Now, he and his wife, Janet Cantwell-Papale, a former world-class gymnast whose own background uniquely mirrors his, are unveiling the secrets to their success.

# Be Invincible!

## A Playbook For Reaching Your Full Potential

*by*
**Vince Papale**
*Subject of the hit Disney Film "Invincible"*
*and*
**Janet Cantwell-Papale**
*with* **Tim Vandehey**

*This book is dedicated to the protectors and defenders
of the American Dream and the preservation
of the values and standards that were so
valiantly fought for by our patriots.*

*Thank you to our paralyzed Vets and
wounded Warriors who defended that dream with valor
and honor, safeguarding it for future generations.*

Published by
VINCE PAPALE PROMOTIONS LLC
Cherry Hill, NJ 08034

Cover Photo credit: Russ Brown / Russ Brown Photography
Cover and page design by Robert DeVitis

Be Invincible! A Playbook For Reaching Your Full Potential
by Vince Papale and Janet Cantwell-Papale

Printed in the United States of America

**These statements have not been evaluated by the Food and Drug Administration. This product is not intended to diagnose, treat, cure or prevent any disease.

# TABLE OF CONTENTS

# *Foreword*

## *by Dick Vermeil, former head coach, Philadelphia Eagles*

When I took the Philadelphia Eagles job in the winter of 1976, I went in knowing that they didn't have a first, second or third round draft pick until 1978. That's three years in a row without quality draft choices, and they hadn't had a winning season in ten years. We were fortunate that back then, there were 17 rounds in the draft instead of the seven they have now, so we would at least gain in numbers. As we went through our early organizational thoughts, we said, "Why don't we host an open tryout in the spring?" We wanted to see if we could pick up a few players who could come in and help us during our ten-week training camp. In 1976 we had six preseason games, so camp was long and tough. You need plenty of bodies to keep intense practice sessions going. Believe me when I say, practices were combative!

The open tryout was a fun (and in some cases, humorous) event. All sizes and shapes showed up. Some had almost no football experience. Some had high school experience. Very few had college experience and a few had been in other training camps. We put those attending through every basic football drill we could without pads on and without killing someone. Only a few appeared to have a little talent. But there was one who that kept jumping out at us in the drills, and when we finally timed them all in the 40-year dash, this guy ran very well. His name was Vince, and when he ran a fast time, we found out his last name was Papale. He had already displayed other athletic movement skills, and now speed. So why not invite him to training camp? Training camp numbers were not limited to 80 like today, so what did we have to lose?

The next step was to interview Vince and find out where he was coming from and what were his expectations. It didn't take long to recognize his passion to play was greater than his talent to play, but when you combined them, there was a slight chance you could end up with a possible contributor. His story was warm, sincere, compassionate and a perfect fit for the Philadelphia environment.

Training camp opened in early July, which is the hot, humid time of the year in the Delaware Valley. A lot of guys quit before they ever gave themselves a shot, but Vince thrived. He got better every day and demonstrated the intensity it would take to end up being a good special teams player. He would get just as tired as everyone else, but would try very hard not to show it. The combination of his athletic skills, passion and work ethic made the evaluation process easy. The only thing we didn't know was how much of what we were seeing would transfer to game day. With six preseason games, he would get a chance to demonstrate how he would handle the pressure of game day competition, and needless to say, he excelled, especially in covering punts and kickoffs.

Vince liked to hit people! It was fun for him and it really made the decision process easier. You don't cover punts and kickoffs live in practice sessions, so the only time we could test him was on game day. I was very glad that he passed the test with flying colors. The coaches couldn't help but root for this kid to make it, and since I had the final say in personnel decisions, I was convinced we had someone who could help us build the foundation we would eventually win with.

It's a good story, and it's also true. It's a story that many could duplicate if they could do things the same way that Vince did, regardless of their endeavor. One of the greatest things a person can be is a good example—an example worthy of emulation. Vince is that, and I'm sure there are many other Vinces out there who just haven't given themselves a chance.

The years have passed, our relationship has matured and Vince's opportunities have expanded due to his ability to take a vision and reinforce it with a value system and a process that would not allow negatives or setbacks to misdirect him. He found a way to invest in the present that would ultimately dictate what his future could become. He's experienced tough times and bad days like we all have—health issues, all the obstacles that most of us face at one time or another. But due to his drive to excel, Vince never used them as excuses to fail. He used them as motivation to succeed. If you get nothing else out of this book, take with you the example of what a person can achieve if he has a passion for excellence guided by common sense and backed with an old-fashioned work ethic.

The problem many people have is that they leave their dreams in a dream state of mind. They don't take those dreams and apply an approach that makes those dreams start coming true. Vince didn't waste his dreams. He made them all come alive. Almost everything he had in mind for his life he has made happen, and you can do the same thing. It is never too late to become the person you aspire to be, do the things you want to do and enjoy the pleasures of life you would like to enjoy. This book won't give you all the answers, but it will provide you with an example of what a person can do if his or her goal means enough.

Vince Papale is an inspiration to me, even now when my coaching career is behind me. I can apply what I have learned from him by using his formula for success in everything else I'm doing today. As Vince says, no matter the changes or challenges, we all have what it takes to be invincible.

Dick Vermeil

# Introduction: I Am, I Said

There is no greater waste than wasted potential, and the greatest challenge to that potential is the constant change we experience. If you cannot adapt and adjust to its ebbs and flows, you are destined to fail in the pursuit of your dream and the fulfillment of your potential. Right now, we're in the middle of the biggest economic earthquake since the Great Depression. People are losing their homes. They are being forced to leave careers they thought they would stay in until retirement and start new jobs. A whole new generation of adults is moving back in with their aging parents because that's the only way everybody can make ends meet.

But change isn't just economic. We're also seeing the rise of technology, from iPads to smart phones, that's changing how we work, communicate and live our daily lives. We're seeing society and families change in ways that are pretty radical, from blended families and gay marriage to the way the government is increasingly invading our private lives in the name of security. No matter what you believe or how you were raised, this might be the most unsettling, disquieting time in American history.

Or not. Every time you open the newspaper or turn on the radio, it seems like you read or hear about somebody who's riding the wave of change with the ease of a pro surfer riding a wave on Oahu's North Shore. You've got entrepreneurs launching new restaurants or tech businesses despite the brutal economy. Unknown authors getting great book deals even in the face of impossible odds. Folks coming back from cancer or divorce or bankruptcy to be happier and healthier than ever before. Maybe you sit back and say, "How in the hell did they do that?" Well, my friend, I'm here to tell you.

It didn't happen by accident. Nobody lucks into success. When I achieved some fame after making the Philadelphia Eagles special teams squad at age 30 back in 1976, plenty of people said I had just gotten a lucky break. But if you know my story, saw the movie *Invincible* or read my book, you know that nothing could be further from the truth. Sure, I came from hard working-class beginnings and didn't play a minute of college football. But I also worked my guts out in tryouts and training camp, learned what my coach, Dick Vermeil, wanted from his players, and found ways to make myself invaluable to the team in the role that suited me best. In other words, I had a plan. When times changed, I had still more plans. I reinvented myself. I became a broadcaster, a trainer and a speaker.

## HAVE A PLAN FOR CHANGING TIMES

This book is all about being prepared for and evolving with changing times, so that you can find the invincibility within yourself and thrive no matter how crazy things around you are becoming. What does it mean to be invincible? It doesn't mean being bulletproof, and it doesn't mean not making any mistakes. Believe me, when I came into the NFL as a raw rookie wide receiver and special teams kamikaze, I made plenty of mistakes. So will you. Change is going to come, probably when you least expect it. Life turns on a dime—sometimes dramatically after a doctor's diagnosis or a pink slip, sometimes subtly with an idea for a new business or an aging parent's forgetfulness. When it does, you have two choices:

## 1. Try to catch up.
## 2. Be prepared.

I believe that 99% of people don't change anything major about their lives until they have no choice. The obese guy doesn't get serious about losing weight until he has his heart attack. The alcoholic doesn't go on the wagon until he wakes up in the drunk tank or gets a DUI. Change is probably going to come into your life without giving you any choice, either. But you can choose to be prepared for it when it does come! Being invincible means having the plan, the character, the support and the strength of mind to deal with whatever changes life throws your way and come out on top.

Being invincible is also about knowing your weaknesses and compensating for them by building up your strengths. It's about understanding that life will throw you some wicked curveballs, but that you can handle them. It's about reinventing yourself constantly and adapting to what comes your way. You're a lot stronger than you think you are. When unemployment, disease or any other challenge comes along, the only thing that can prevent you from meeting and beating that challenge is you.

It's also about having a plan. When things change, some people are going to panic or freeze like a deer in the headlights of an SUV. You know what happens to that deer, right? Splat. If you're inflexible or believe that you can only survive under certain conditions, you're going to be helpless when big changes hit. But if you have a plan that keeps you thinking positive, taking care of your body and mind, and developing new skills, you'll be ready to find opportunities where other people only find fear.

That's being tougher than the times. If you don't believe that you have that kind of resiliency in you—even if you've never believed it—now is the time to start.

## NEIL DIAMOND IS MY GURU

When I was younger, the Neil Diamond song, "I Am, I Said," lifted me up more than any other song I had ever heard. You know the tune:

*I am, I said*
*To no one there*
*And no one heard at all*
*Not even the chair*

To a young guy who had come out of the projects of suburban Philadelphia and dreamed of playing pro football but had accepted that he would spend his life as a schoolteacher, Neil was singing about me. The song was about someone who, even though he had great potential inside, had always been invisible to everyone around him. I decided that I wouldn't allow that to happen to me. I would show everyone what kind of man I was.

Let me tell you, there's nothing exceptional about me. Just like when I was a player, I was and always will be a blue-collar guy with a blue-collar attitude. To this day, people tell me that I never forgot where I'm from and I take great pride in that. Ask me what I'm made of and I'd say that I'm all heart and truth and guts, no finesse. I made the Eagles, stayed in the NFL and won the hearts of the people of Philadelphia because I brought unlimited passion to the field every single day and played like I was out of my mind on every single play. Why not? I did something that I think more people should do if they want real success in their lives:

1. I found something that I loved doing.
2. I determined what I needed to do to keep doing it.
3. I did that something to the best of my ability every single moment.

That's not rocket science, right? Good, because I'm no rocket scientist. I'm a guy who now, in my mid-sixties, makes a living speaking to big groups and companies about the lessons I've learned in my life. That's why I, along with my wonderful wife Janet, have written this book. I'm going to share with you my secrets to becoming invincible in your own life, no matter how tough the times may get.

Joining me in this is my wife, Janet Cantwell Papale, who's the strongest and most capable woman I've ever known. A former world-class gymnast who reinvented herself as a world-class diver after a career-ending knee injury, she's lived the lessons of this book as a successful coach at The University of Pennsylvania, an entrepreneur and real estate professional, and a wife and mother. Janet amazes me every day by managing my career, taking care of our family and still inspiring everyone around her. She's got plenty to share with you throughout these pages.

I think we've made it pretty clear when either Janet or I are speaking. When we switch from one to the other, you'll see one of our names in capital letters—JANET:—in front of a new section. When we switch back to me, you'll see my name—VINCE:—at the start of a new section. It should be clear. Janet also has some fantastic candid opinions and advice just for women; you'll find them in the "Janet's Words for Women" sidebars in each chapter.

## YOUR INVINCIBLE MOMENT

If there's one thing you can say about me and Janet, it's that we're survivors. I've survived growing up on the outskirts of the toughest city in America. I've survived Coach Vermeil's infamously brutal training camps and the bone-crushing grind of the NFL. And I've survived colon cancer, which doctors were fortunate enough to detect early.

Janet survived Lyme disease and a terrible sledding accident where she was actually in the hospital getting last rites. She survived the end of her gymnastics dream and came back stronger, first as a outstanding diver (now that's an incredible athlete!) and then as a top coach. But we're really not that special. There's nothing in us that's not in you, too.

That's exactly why when I was playing football, it seemed like the whole city of Philly came out to cheer me on game days. It's the same reason that even now, people come up to me and tell me that my career or my movie inspired them or helped them through a dark time in their lives. I'm one of them. I was the real Rocky. People see something in me that they also have in themselves. We all have it. You have it. You just need to see it and use it.

Janet and I are going to tell you how to do that. We'll tell you how to make your plan. We'll advise you on how to set and change your goals as life changes. We'll talk about how to understand and define your role. We'll tell you how to avoid the "bucket of crabs." We'll share with you the fitness and nutrition secrets that keep us looking younger and feeling better than a lot of folks twenty years younger. And that's just for starters. You'll learn everything you need to create your own invincible moment—that time when you defied the odds and your own limitations, silenced the doubters and overcame your fears to come out on top.

We're also going to share with you some stories from real people who have had their own Invincible Moments: a few celebrities and a lot of regular Americans who have faced down some of life's most difficult changes and won. These are people who have beaten cancer, survived bankruptcy and recovered from personal tragedies by showing courage and an ability to adapt that they never realized they had. Throughout this book, we'll reveal some of their stories, which will inspire and amaze you. Let me tell you, they are the real heroes.

## YOU'VE GOT TO BELIEVE

Janet and I are going to pass on a lot of good advice during our time together. But none of it is as important as our very first piece of advice: Nothing begins until you believe. Until you believe that you can overcome an obstacle, achieve a dream or defy the people who said you'd never amount to anything, you're going nowhere. Believe me, I know. When my first wife left me, she left a note in our cleaned-out house that read, "You'll never go anywhere, never make a name for yourself, and never make any money."

For a while, I believed her. I moped. I sulked. I cried. While I was doing that, I really did go nowhere. It was only when I started realizing she was wrong—when I believed that I could be more than a frustrated would-be decathlete and never-was football star—that I started taking confident, concrete steps to make my pro football dreams into realities.

Until you believe, there's no one who can help you. Once you believe, there's no one who can stop you. Belief is the first step. I think that's why my story has stayed in people's minds more than 30 years after my last NFL game: It gives them hope that great things are not impossible. I have a friend, a former NFL player, who a few years back kept taking injections for a tumor in his arm. Eventually, he lost the arm. His doctors and friends all insisted that, among other things, he would never be able to tie a necktie again.

So what, right? Well, that necktie became for him the symbol of proving all the people who said, "You can't" wrong. These days he's a speaker like me, and he tells that story to his audiences…while taking off his necktie and retying it in a perfect Windsor knot with one hand. It's fantastic.

In the movie *Invincible*, Mark Wahlberg, who plays me, messes up against the Dallas Cowboys, goes over to the bench and all the other players move away from him like he's got the plague. Well, I got a letter once from a woman who has two autistic children, and when the kids go to the lunch table everybody moves away from them because her kids behave strangely. She told me that her family loves that scene from the movie because it helped them overcome the shame and frustration they feel when other people shun their little ones. It just doesn't bother them anymore.

One of the best examples of belief came from a twelve-year-old boy named Alex I once met. He was confined to a wheelchair, and he told his mother that *Invincible* was his favorite movie because, he said, "They told Vince he couldn't make the team and they all told me I couldn't walk again. But Vince made the team and I'm going to walk again." Talk about being brave in the face of a terrible change! I don't doubt for a second that he will walk again with an attitude like that.

## STICK WITH PEOPLE WHO SUPPORT YOU

That's belief strong enough to bring tears to your eyes. That's the first ingredient in becoming invincible: believing that you can do it. If you're at that point, and you know there's something better beyond the hard times, the layoff notices, the sleepless nights and the worries, then you're ready.

One word of caution.  When you start becoming invincible, changing your life and making good things happen, you'll probably find some people you know resenting you.  I know because it happened to me. I was a hero to 95% of Philadelphia when I made the Eagles squad, especially to the other "knuckleheads" I'd drank and cheered with up in the 700 section of old Veterans Stadium.  Sure, there were some players who didn't like all the press I was getting as an unproven rookie.  NFL safety Ken Reeves said to me, "I'm going to knock your damned head off, Papale.  I've been in this league for thirteen years and I just saw your story on NBC."  I went to the official and warned him that Reeves was out to get me, but later in the game he clocked me right under my chin so hard that my gum flew out.  That's the NFL for you.

But I expected that sort of thing and worked to avoid drawing attention to myself as much as possible.  What hurt more than the jealous players were the fans and friends who were jealous of the attention I was getting.  They apparently hated me for achieving something that they had maybe dreamed about but never gone for.  At first, I was stunned and hurt by the angry words and the accusations that I was now a stuck-up NFL hotshot.  But I realized that it wasn't about me; it was about them.

You can't worry about those people.  Account for them but ignore them.  Your opinion—and the opinions of the people who really love you and stand by you no matter what—matter most.  They will all be a source of strength and inspiration.  Because once you believe, and once you have a plan in place, you're invincible.

Let's start training camp.  It won't be as rough as a Dick Vermeil session, but it'll get you in great shape for a successful life.

# CHAPTER ONE

# WHAT'S YOUR VISION
## AND WHAT
# DOES IT COST?

*"Happy are those who dream dreams and are willing to pay the price to make them come true."*

— Leo Jozef Suenens

The quote left is from a plaque that George Corner, my coach and mentor at Interboro High School in Philadelphia, gave me one day. George was more than a mentor for me—he was a father figure at a time when my mother was sinking into mental illness and my dad was either caring for her or working his butt off with little time to pay attention to me. When my mom was taken to the hospital in a straitjacket, George confided in me that mental illness also ran in his own family. He knew that I needed to know I wasn't alone in this. He was the only adult in my life at the time I could really talk to. I wanted and needed to talk with my Dad, but mistakenly thought he wouldn't listen.

George was also the person responsible for my vision of myself as a football player. I excelled in basketball and track in school, but I didn't play football (other than youth football) because even though I was the fastest kid around, I was small: 5 feet, 6 inches tall as a high school senior and only 145 pounds soaking wet. But when he became the football coach before my senior year, he invited me to try out for the team. I trained like a maniac, learned everything I could about being a wide receiver, and made the team over kids who had been playing their guts out since Pop Warner ball. With that, even though I ended up going to St. Joseph's College on a track scholarship, I had a vision: I was a football player.

The quote on that plaque (which, incidentally, comes from a former Catholic archbishop) told me much that I needed to know about life. First of all, having a dream or vision was critical to happiness. Second, my vision would come with a price. Finally and most important, paying that price should be enjoyable for me. That didn't mean it would be easy, but don't we get the most joy out of the things we work hardest to achieve? I think so. That idea helped set me on a course that would ultimately lead to the Philadelphia Eagles and the life I have today.

## THERE ARE NO SHORT CUTS

Do you have a vision for your life? If you don't, then you're basically bumping from one thing to the next like a pinball (if you're a boomer like me and remember pinball machines, that is). There's an old saying that goes, "A goal is a dream with a plan." My version is, "A vision is a goal with a price tag." That means that while you need a strong vision of what you want your future to look like, you also need to be prepared to deal with some serious consequences of pursuing it.  Because you get what you pay for.  The higher the price of your vision, the greater respect and care you're going to give your achievement.

I'll give you an example.  Think about the people you know who have lost weight by doing one fad diet or another.  Now think about the ones who've lost weight by changing how they ate and putting in the hours at the gym, on the bike or at the running track.  Of the people in the first group, how many of them maintained their weight loss over a long period of time?  Probably not many, right?  That's because it didn't cost them much.  They had a vision of being thin, but they didn't want to pay the high cost, which was changing how they thought and behaved.  So the vision came to pass…temporarily.  But it didn't stick.  Because the vision didn't come with a high cost, it was easy to disrespect it, lose discipline and slide back into bad habits.

Now, what about the folks who lost weight by eating smart and work-ing out?  Their results came more slowly.  It seemed like they were always sweating it out on the exercise bike or the squat rack, right?  Yet have most of them maintained their improved weight and fitness?  I'll bet they have.  They were willing to pay the higher cost of doing things right.  In return, they changed how they ate, how they moved, how they thought about food—whatever worked for them.  The cost was high, but the results last.

### *Your vision is worth exactly what it costs you to make it a reality.*

Here's another way to think of this.  If you take karate classes diligently for years, you will eventually earn your black belt.  That means you will proba-bly have the physical skill and fitness to win a fight with almost anyone on the street.  However, part of the process of becoming a karate master is developing calmness, wisdom and mental discipline, so by the time you earn your black belt you will also have become the kind of person who does not need to fight.  The cost of realizing your vision will always be changing not only what you do, but who you are.  If you can't accept that cost, your vision will probably always be just a dream.  If you take short cuts you might achieve what you want for a while, but because you're still the same person as when you started, it won't last.

**JANET:** Another fact is that your vision constantly gets redefined as life throws you new things. The vision I had for my life at 16 years old—being a gymnast—was different from the vision I had as a coach and businessperson. You can't get locked into a single vision, because what you thought was a prior-

ity in your younger years all of a sudden doesn't mean anything to you when you're 40 and what you care about is completely different.

Believe me, as a coach you see it all the time: young athletes who have the talent but not the drive. I'm not just talking about gymnastics, but any sport. It's one thing to aspire to be a pro or an Olympian when you're 14 and have nothing else in your life. It's something else to be 22 and have a hundred choices in front of you. Plenty of talented athletes go another direction and don't look back at sports because they decide it isn't as important as they once thought. There's nothing wrong with it; if you don't have it in you to make the sacrifices that sports demands, then don't be an athlete. But that illustrates how what you thought you wanted more than anything can change.

## MY VISION AND ITS COST

**VINCE:** You already know that my vision or dream was to play professional football. I knew I had the athletic ability to be successful, but no pro in any sport ever made it on talent alone. The competition is just too intense for that. I knew that if I was going to play any sort of ball with my limited resume, I needed three things: experience, refined football skills and to be in the best shape of my life.

I could only get the first two, unfortunately, by playing at a high level. Rough touch games weren't going to cut it. That meant when the Philadelphia Bell of the new World Football League came calling, I answered. I was 28 years old and teaching, but I knew this might be my only chance to get some reps at the pro level. There's simply no substitute for training with other pros and playing with real games at stake. It's the best classroom around. So I left my regular classroom and spent a month training more intensely than ever before.  I hung out with former San Diego Chargers wideout Ron Holliday and picked up pointers on how to be a pro wide receiver—things I would have learned years before had I played college ball, but hadn't.

When I made the Bell and later made the Eagles, the cost of my vision started to become very clear: exhausting work in training camp, injuries (including the shoulder injury that would eventually end my career in 1979), and the hardest work I had ever done in my life.  See, I knew that I wasn't a polished NFL player with skills honed over years.  I was as raw as a rare piece of filet mignon.  So I made up for it by working so hard and playing with such total disregard for my own safety that Coach Vermeil thought I was a little nuts.  I took pride in that.  But it took a toll on my body.  It took a toll on relationships, too.

**JANET:** The thing is, Vince has always been about more than football.  When we were doing the movie Invincible, I told him we were going to go to ICM, one of the most powerful talent agencies in the world, and get him on television.  He said, "I don't like TV, I don't want to be a sports anchor." He'd had a terrible experience at WCAU Channel 10 after getting out of football.  He had the top-rated weekend sports program in the fourth-largest market in the country, but he got no support.  He would work from 8:30 in the morning to midnight and get hammered by his producer.  Because of that negative experience, Vince didn't see himself being on television again.

It took a lot of convincing to get him out of that mindset to where he could envision himself doing a TV show.  Now he does a show for the Eagles and is completely comfortable in front of a camera.  That just shows you that your vision of yourself has to change with time.  If you have only one idea of who and what you can be, you're going to miss a lot of opportunities.

**VINCE:** Those experiences made me a different person.  I was more disciplined.  I was in fantastic physical shape thanks to habits that I still maintain to this day.  I had a new awareness of my power to inspire the regular blue-collar folks of Philly—and the enormous responsibility that came with that power.  Those changes have changed who I am today, and they've lasted because I paid a high price to make them happen.  Was it worth it? You bet your life it was.

# INVINCIBLE MOMENT

*When he was 12, Jason Lester was struck by a car and lost the use of his right arm. Formerly a gifted baseball player whose father had him on the fast track to the pros, Jason was faced with trying to prove that he could play all over again with one arm. "Everyone laughed at me for trying out for baseball the year after losing the use of my arm," he says. "Not only did I play, I started and made All-Stars. That was the moment I knew would never stop following my dream of being the best. I started running at 15 to slim down and found my gift for endurance racing."*

*Jason's motto is "Never Stop," and it has served him well as he has built a career as an ultra-endurance athlete, completing Ironman and Ultraman (a double-length Ironman) triathlons and other extreme distance races and writing his first book. But nothing could have prepared him for the challenge of EPIC5, an event that he created. Consisting of 5 Ironman triathlons on 5 consecutive days on 5 different Hawaiian islands, it was a daunting task even for an able-bodied athlete. Jason faced it while also acting as chief event organizer and after suffering a personal loss on the eve of the event. Because his damaged right arm slows him in a triathlon's swim stage, he found himself at the back of the pack of athletes, often biking and running alone in the dark in the wee hours of the morning. The isolation, emotional anguish, physical pain and utter exhaustion of such a feat could easily have broken anyone.*

*But Jason didn't stop. On the morning of May 10, hours after the last finisher had come in, he ran up Ali'i Drive in Kailua-Kona, Hawaii, knelt and kissed the ground, and bounced back up with a broad grin. He had created and completed the world's most difficult endurance race at the same time. Epic.*

## DREAMING AIN'T DOING

A vision is about seeing what your life can be in the future and then taking steps to make that future come to pass. Your vision should become the guiding force in your life, the theme that drives everything else. It's like that vision becomes a template that everything else you do needs to fit into. If you're presented with an option, you ask, Does it fit into my vision? If the answer is no, you don't pursue it. That's how having a strong, clear vision shapes your future and your present.

Without a vision, you're just marking time. John Lennon wrote, "Life is what happens while you're busy making other plans," but what happens when you don't have any plans? Life passes you by. You have nothing to work towards. Your vision is your blueprint for tomorrow.

That's why I worry when I hear people talking about their dreams. I'm tempted to reply, "That's great, what are you doing about it?" Because a dream without a vision for how to make it come true is nothing. Dreamers are not necessarily doers. There are plenty of posers out there who make excuses for not fulfilling their dreams. It's important not to kid yourself into believing that you've actually accomplished something just because you have a dream or set a goal. You haven't. If all I'd done was pat myself on the back for aspiring to play pro football after I left St. Joseph's, that would have gotten me exactly no closer to actually doing it. Having a dream or vision is necessary, but it's only the first step. It's like packing for a long trip. You need to do it, but if all you do after that is set your suitcases on the front porch and expect the plane to fly by and pick you up, you won't get anywhere.

### JANET'S WORDS FOR WOMEN

*With feminism, we fought for equality but all we did was add things on. We still have all the same nurturing female instincts. So now you have women who maintain careers and still cook and keep the house. It's rare that you have a woman anymore who does just one thing. So it's especially important as a woman to know what your vision is, because some choices don't give you*

> *do-overs. I know a lot of female professionals. They build their careers, then hit their 40s and say, "Now I want to have kids." But sometimes they can't. That ship has sailed. Figure out what you want and if kids are part of it, make sure you make time. Not everybody can have their last kid at 44 like I did.*

Every so often, you'll see someone "make it" to the top without having any sort of clear vision, just based on incredible talent. The trouble with this is that the person hasn't developed the character or discipline to stay at the top. This happens all the time in sports, where gifted players often start attracting attention from agents and sponsors while they're in junior high school, for heaven's sake.

In my sport, a great example of this was a young quarterback drafted by the San Diego Chargers in 1998. Some teams thought seriously about taking him above Peyton Manning. But he quickly proved to be what coaches call a "head case": hard to coach, unwilling to work, hot-tempered and stubborn. He allegedly lied about injuries so he could skip player symposiums or play golf, and refused surgery on an injured wrist despite many recommendations from doctors. He retired in 2002 and is considered to be one of the biggest busts in sports history.

How does something like that happen? Talent. This guy was obviously an incredible college football talent without a vision of what he would do once he reached the NFL. He faked it, tried to improvise and thought he could take short cuts. Not in the pros, buddy. If you don't put in the work, your teammates will hate you, the opposing team will bury you and your coaches will cut you.

The lesson: To succeed you need a vision, ability and a plan of action. If you're lacking any one of them, you'll be on the sidelines.

> **INVINCIBLE WISDOM**
>
> *"If you only do what you know you can do, you never do very much."*
>
> — *Tom Krause*

## WHAT'S YOUR VISION?

So what's your vision for your future? How do you see yourself adapting to the changing times? In the chapters to come, I'm going to talk about a wide range of skills and mental disciplines that you can use to help you adjust to changes and be at your best no matter what opportunities come along. But they're useless unless you have a strong vision for what you want from the next five, ten or 30 years and a plan to make that vision happen.

So let's talk about your vision. I've created a little plan to help you figure out what it is, so if you like, grab a sheet of paper or your laptop and take notes as we go. First of all, the goal here is to come away with three things:

**1. A vision.** Close your eyes and see yourself doing what you want to do and being where you want to be. Feel it.

**2. A plan.** Write down the steps you need to follow to make your vision happen.

**3. An idea of the cost and how you'll pay it.**

When it comes to your vision, you're probably not starting from zero. Most of us have at least a vague idea of what we want our lives to look like in ten years. The problem is the vague part. Many people don't have enough detail. You want to have your own business? Great. What kind of business? Located where? Making how much money? How will you start it? There are so many questions to answer that the whole process can be intimidating, but every time you come up with an answer, it gets easier.

Let's start there. Visualize what you want your life to look like in five years, ten years and 20 years. See all the details in your mind: what you'll look like, where you'll be living, what you'll be doing, who you'll be spending your time with and more. Be as specific as you can be and write everything down. This isn't some sort of New Age nonsense; I'm not going to sit here and tell you that if you breathe through your third eye you can make your dreams come true. But if you don't visualize the details, you can't come up with a plan for making them a reality.

One thing I absolutely recommend that you do when you're writing down your vision is be daring, if that's what you want. You might have a great life going and only want to keep it going, saving money for retirement and having your kids turn out happy. That's great. But if you have a big dream, don't talk yourself out of going for it! As long as you're not aiming for something that's completely impossible (like making the NFL at 65), don't worry about other people telling you your dream is too big. Everything is impossible until you try it. Don't be afraid to dream big.

That brings me to step two: have a plan. Break down your vision step by step. What do you have to do first? Second? What about after that? If your vision is launching your own restaurant, your first step might be to figure out your menu. If it's to make a college football team when you're an AARP member, your first step had better be to have a physical. Map out the path you'll need to take to get from start to finish, and then have a plan for completing each of those steps.

This is definitely a part of the book where I encourage you to take your time. You might not know all the steps that go into making your vision a reality, especially if it's something like starting a small business or becoming a lawyer. So do your research. Talk to mentors. Learn what you need to know and slowly build your plan.

**JANET:** Taking your time is especially important right now. We live in a time of instant gratification. Everybody wants his vision to come to pass right now, and life doesn't work that way. Too many people are losing their sense of what a vision is: a long-term roadmap for your life. It takes time to for all the pieces to come together. Patience is part of the price of a vision. You've got to have faith that if you do the right things, act according to your character and ethics, and treat people well, eventually things will fall into place. They usually will, but it's not going to happen overnight.

**VINCE:** The final part of the equation is know the cost. Remember, the quote said that the lucky ones were the people who can or are willing to pay the cost of their dreams. Dreams worth having aren't free. They come with a price tag, and you should love paying that bill. Wait a minute? Didn't I work myself to death in Coach Vermeil's training camp when I was trying to make the Eagles, and kill myself in practice and on game days? Yes, but I loved it. It was brutal punishment, but it was part of the whole experience of doing something I loved, so I loved doing it. I may have hated walking out of practice so dehydrated that I could barely stand, but I loved being there. I loved my place in the world.

That's what I want you to do as you prepare for life's changes. Find a vision you can fall in love with, anticipate what it's going to cost, and know that you're willing to pay that cost. Want to do an Ironman triathlon? Great. The cost will be months of grueling training and buying a $5,000 bike. Want to win American Idol? Fantastic. The cost will be voice

*Whatever edge I could get to go light and gain speed ... QB shoulder pads with leather and felt pads. No wonder my career ended abruptly with shoulder injuries.*

and performance lessons, one nerve-wracking audition after another, crushing pressure and the constant threat of TV humiliation.

Plan for the cost of your vision just like you plan for the cost of buying a house. Budget what you're going to be able to handle. Just as important, know what you'll do when things go right and when they go wrong. Take it from me—your trip to your vision won't always be smooth. When you hit a setback, how will you handle it? Who will you talk to and how will you bounce back?

How will you handle success? When I got my first bonus check from the Eagles, I went shopping for a decent suit. That's pretty home-spun, simple stuff. But sports and entertainment are full of stories about overnight sensations who get their first big payday, blow everything on big houses and stupid investments, and wind up broke. Have a plan for handling success. It's just as important as knowing how to handle obstacles.

## END ZONE

**Things to think about & do after finishing this chapter**

- Write down and refine your vision for the next five, ten and 20 years.
- Write down all the steps you need to follow to make it happen.
- Write down the cost and how you'll pay it.
- Share your vision with people so you know who will support you in tough times and who you can't count on.
- Find examples of people who have achieved amazing personal visions to inspire you when the going gets tough.

**Q: What's your vision?**

A: _____

**Q: What steps do you need to take to make it happen?**

**Q: What resources will you need?**

**Q: What people will you need?**

Step 1: _____

Step 2: _____

Step 3: _____

Step 4: _____

Step 5: _____

Step 6: _____

Resources: _____

People: _____

# CHAPTER TWO

# NOBODY PLANS TO FAIL, THEY FAIL TO PLAN

*"Good fortune is what happens when opportunity meets with planning."*

— Thomas Edison

When I was gunning for a spot on the Eagles, I was running on a mixture of hope, adrenaline and nothing-to-lose passion. But I also had a plan. You don't go into something that crazy and demanding without a plan or the rigors of an NFL tryout and training camp will chew you up and spit you out.

After I made the team, that didn't change. It wasn't like I had signed some sort of multi-year guaranteed contract; I was season-to-season, game-to-game and practice-to-practice and could be cut at any time. I was a marginal as a player could be. There were no days off. If I wanted to stay, I needed a plan to continue proving my value. Part of that plan was to get in the best physical condition I could. I had always been a fiend for working out, and I still am today, which is one of the reasons that in my mid-sixties I look better than a lot of guys in their mid-forties. But back in those days, year-round fitness was just not on the radar for a lot of guys. They figured that they spent the entire NFL preseason and regular season getting pounded, working out and trying to stay healthy, so by God they were going to relax in the offseason. I swear there were some players on some teams who didn't set foot in a gym or on a running track from the final play of the last game to the first drills of the following year's training camp, and it showed. You could tell they came to training camp to get in shape.

You couldn't do that with Dick Vermeil. He bragged about his players being the best conditioned in the league, and the team designed personalized fitness programs for every guy. He also singled me out as the best conditioned of the Eagles. Wow, no pressure, Coach. I figured if I lived up to that assessment, I would have the best shot at having a job. I also didn't want to go through the kind of hell I had in the 1976 training camp.

So after the '76 season I worked out like a demon. Denny Franks and I actually showed up at Veterans Stadium on January 2, 1977 to work out, until the athletic trainers kicked us out. That didn't stop me. I pumped iron until I'd boosted my bench press from 180 pounds to 296. I went into the 1977 season in incredible shape and wound up signing contracts for 1977, '78 and '79. My plan paid off.

## POTENTIAL TAKES PLANNING

Vince Lombardi said, "Potential is something you ain't done yet." As mentioned earlier, mankind's greatest waste is wasted potential; that's what comes back to haunt us at night when we're not living the kind of life we could have lived. Potential is basically raw talent, but without refinement and polishing it's really not good for much. That's where planning comes in. No matter how much potential you have, if you don't have a plan to develop it and do something with it, it's probably going to go to waste. It's a myth that you can sit around all your life and just "be discovered" one day; if you want something, you have to go after it.

**JANET:** You have to be your own advocate and have a plan to make things happen. Vince's whole life changed because he spoke up. He had always been a people pleaser and non-confrontational, but that meant he'd lost out on some opportunities. But when he was trying out for the Philadelphia Bell, and they were getting ready to cut him from the second round of camp, he spoke up. It turned out that they wanted the fastest guys and though Vince had run a 4.5 second 40-yard dash, they didn't believe it. So he challenged them, they timed him again and voila! He stayed in camp. If he hadn't done that, he would never have made the Bell or the Eagles. You have to have a plan and be assertive about opening your mouth, or life will pass you by and you'll resent it or feel sorry for yourself.

**VINCE:** I was speaking to a college graduating class and the three takeaways I gave them were potential, opportunity and impact. First, figure out what your potential is. Then work hard to create opportunities and have a plan to take advantage of them. Finally, find a way that you can turn your potential into impact that makes a positive difference for somebody.

In football, I recognized my own potential first: I knew I was fast and had athletic ability as well as the passion to play harder than anyone. Fine, but without opportunity that would have been all I had. So I had a plan: go out for the Philly team in the new pro league, make it, get noticed and get a tryout with the Eagles. That all panned out for me. I made it stick by turning it into positive impact. First, I stayed humble and grateful and became a working-class hero for the people of a city that was down-and-out at the time. Later, when I survived colon cancer, I made an impact by leveraging my

14

celebrity to raise awareness about the disease and money for research.

You've got to have a game plan. In the last chapter, we talked about having a vision or a goal for your life. Start there. But after you have it in your mind, you've only taken one step toward it. Now you need a step-by-step plan. Begin with the goal in mind and work backward. Look at the big, major steps you need to take in order to reach your goal. Now move back and consider the smaller steps you need to take to get to the big steps.

For example, let's say you're a corporate cubicle dweller and you want to start your own business. That's the end point. Work backward from there. Figure out the steps you need to take to make that dream happen. Once you've figured those out, work out the smaller steps that will get you to the bigger steps. For example, you want to get investors. Fine, but before you can do that you need a business plan and a prototype. You need partners. You need to network and build relationships that can turn into partnerships, money and ideas.

You might come up with four tiers of steps you have to follow, but that's fine. That's the inevitable groundwork that we've all got to do. It's not glamorous, but as long as you have discipline and keep working your plan, you'll move from one tier (networking events) to the next (private pitch meetings with investors) to the next (signing contracts to start your company with your partners in key positions). Before you know it you've hit your goal and done all the preparation along the way to make sure you stay there and get the greatest benefit from all your hard work.

## JANET'S WORDS FOR WOMEN

*Women are multi-taskers; men typically aren't. That's why we sit down while men stand up. We're planning! Men are linear and need to do one thing at a time, but women can go from point A to point K to point X without getting confused. That's just the way we're wired. Take advantage, ladies. Your plan should be more flexible than a man's and take advantage of the fact that you can do many things simultaneously. That lets you be incredibly productive.*

# IF YOU DON'T HAVE A PLAN...

Following a plan takes a ridiculous amount of discipline. In his classic book *Good to Great*, Jim Collins writes that the key factor behind the success of the eleven companies he designated as great was "disciplined people, disciplined thought and disciplined action." What is discipline? To my mind, it's having a plan and then following that plan no matter what is happening around you. Of course it's important to be flexible and adaptable and I'll get to that in a little while, but for now, let's look at the importance of being disciplined...and what can happen when you aren't.

> ### INVINCIBLE WISDOM
>
> *"Three rules for coaching: Surround yourself with people who can't live without football. Recognize winners; they come in all forms. Have a plan for everything."*
>
> — Bear Bryant

In Alice in Wonderland, Lewis Carroll wrote, "If you don't know where you're going, any road will take you there." If you don't have a plan, it's impossible to be disciplined. You'll do whatever looks good at the time, and most of the time that's not going to be what's good for you in the long run. What if you decide on a whim—without a plan—that this is the year you'll start that business and you impulsively quit your job? In this economy, that might not be such a wise move. If you haven't done the planning and background work, odds are your venture will fail and there you'll be—unemployed.

A plan is like a filtering device for sorting through all the opportunities and people that come your way. If you have a plan, when someone comes to you with an idea or proposal, you can say to yourself, "Does it fit into the plan?" If it doesn't, then politely pass. If it does, great. Being disciplined saves you a lot of wasted time and effort and keeps you focused on the things you need to do. But it's not easy.

Life is full of distractions and temptations. Sometimes, people will try to distract you because they don't want you to achieve something that will make them feel bad about themselves. Other times, apparent shortcuts will appear and you'll have to resist taking them. When you have a plan in mind and a firm commitment to seeing it through, step by step, you're much more likely to ignore the well-meaning friends telling you to skip a few workouts ("You don't really want to run a marathon, do you?") or the buddy with a surefire business idea who needs you to be his CFO.

Without a plan, you're depending on blind luck to carry you through, and that usually means you're doomed to failure. With a plan, there still aren't any guarantees but you improve your odds of being able to turn your potential into real success and happiness.

## WHO'S YOUR OPPONENT?

One of the great things about sports is that it seems like knowing your opponent is easy. It's the other team or the other player, right? For Janet, when she was competing as a gymnast and when she was coaching at Penn, the opponent was always the other team or university. For me, the opponent was whoever I lined up against at scrimmage on a punt or kickoff. Sports makes it seem easy to identify who you're up against and to figure out what you've got to do to beat the enemy. Simple, right?

*That's Janet Cantwell, the underdog, grabbing the Gold Medal for the vault at the National Intercollegiate Gymnastics Championships when she was 18 years old."*

Except that it's not that simple. Sure, it might look like the only opponent out there is the other team, but it's not always obvious who your real opponent is. When you're trying to carry out a plan for your life or career, you're going to run into opposition. If you're going to be successful you should know who your opponent is and how to defeat it.

Sometimes, your opponent will be yourself. If you're full of self-doubt or negativity, or you have a bad attitude or no discipline, then you're going to sabotage yourself at every turn. Fear is the great enemy.

17

It can paralyze you. If you're a gymnast, you won't be your best if you're afraid out on the floor. You have to know your fears, worries, anxieties and doubts before you start trying to carry out your plan, so that you can keep them from stopping you. If you do that, you can have a support system in place to keep you on track. That might be your spouse, friends, a therapist, a personal trainer, whatever. It doesn't matter. Knowing your opponent lets you prepare.

Or maybe your opponent is something else:

- **Friends or family—** The people we love can exert a lot of pressure on us to do or not do things a certain way.

- **The culture—** Are there things in your ethnic or religious tradition that simply are not done? The culture you grew up in—or even the town you grew up in—can limit you if you let it.

- **The economy—** Let's face it, the economic upheaval of the last few years has put a lot of dreams on hold. Sometimes, when things are rough and times are changing fast, the best you can do is work on your plan, try not to lose ground and be ready when things turn around. Or you are forced to attempt your dream because you get a pink slip and have no other choice.

- **Your health—** Your body may limit you, especially if your goal is an athletic one like doing an Ironman. Make a plan with your healthcare team to safely get the most you can from what you've got.

If you know the kind of resistance you're likely to hit, you can create plans and find tools to get past it and still get to your goals. If you don't, then you're like a blind boxer.

## INVINCIBLE MOMENT

Ed Harrold shares his Invincible Moment with us:

"The event was a 22-mile swim around Atlantic City. The year was 1996, and I was a local boy, born and raised in Ventnor, New Jersey. I was 35 years old, the oldest guy to ever try the swim at that time. I was also an amateur swimmer in a field of 28 professional, international-caliber swimmers.

"The water temperature was in the 50s—freezing cold. For the first few miles everything was okay, but I spent the next few miles vomiting. I couldn't keep anything down. For the next few miles I wanted to quit and get into my support boat a million times, but I didn't. I hung tough. Then, at about 16 miles into the race, my ego finally let go. The pain and agony finally went away and my mind went blank. The water in the back bays on Ventnor City got a little warmer and I found something inside myself I never knew existed until that day.

"It was an energy source. It was amazing and powerful, with the deepest of meditation and focus. I was in the zone. I saw that there is a bottomless supply of energy inside each of us that we can tap when our egos get out of the way and let our bodies do their thing. I swam the final six miles in a dead sprint, an effortless 90 strokes a minute.

"I finished the race pumped, in front of thousands of fans at the dock bar at Harrah's Casino. Afterward, some of the other crews came up to me and asked me what it was like swimming under the final bridge, the Brigantine Bridge, into the tide that was running in at seven miles an hour...while I was only swimming six miles an hour! It turned out that all 13 swimmers who finished before me were allowed to hold on to the back of their support boats without being disqualified. I came in last in 14th place; the rest of the pros dropped out due to the brutal conditions.

"So I was the only person to actually swim the race by the rules without holding on to the back of the boat and being towed under the bridge."

## CALL AN AUDIBLE

In football, when players line up at scrimmage there's already a play on that the quarterback has laid down in the huddle. But if the team lines up and sees that something about the opponent is different—they are planning to blitz, for instance—then the quarterback or another player can call an audible. That's a shouted verbal signal to change the play on the fly. It's improvisation in the face of changing conditions. That's also a part of successful planning.

A while back, I said that you should have the discipline to stick with the steps of your plan no matter what's going on around you. That's still true, but with a qualification. When people are trying to turn you aside from your goal or get rich quick schemes threaten to distract you from what you're trying to achieve, by all means be steadfast and stay with your plan. But when the underlying conditions change, it's crucial to be able to call an audible, to have a Plan B.

For example, let's go back to the corporate employee who aspires to start her own company. Maybe she's got a two-year plan to save money, write her business plan, refine her products, learn more about her market, line up some customers and develop her brand. That's fantastic—but then, the rules change. A company in the same niche that she wants to fill goes out of business, leaving hundreds of customers out in the cold. That's a time to audible! Maybe she accelerates her plans, borrows money from her parents and launches her company in two months, not two years, to capitalize on the opportunity. By doing so, she's taking advantage of changing conditions that wouldn't exist if she stuck stubbornly to her plans and waited.

Calling an audible isn't for everyone. Some people are not good at improvising. They feel more comfortable sticking to a set plan because they have a greater sense of control. If that's you, that's okay. You shouldn't get so far out of your comfort zone that you're too terrified to do anything. But as you're making your plans, take a personal inventory of your ability to improvise. Under what circumstances could you call an audible, and under what circumstances would you always hang with your original plan?

It's also smart to formulate a Plan B. If X happens, can you do Y?

If it you injure your leg and can't be ready for the marathon you've always wanted to run, can you do a half-marathon instead? If you can't pass the bar exam after multiple tries, is there something else you could do with that law degree while you're waiting a few

> INVINCIBLE WISDOM
>
> *"It takes as much energy to wish as it does to plan."*
>
> — *Eleanor Roosevelt*

years to give the test another shot? This isn't planning for failure, and it's not the dreaded "something to fall back on." It's being mature and smart. Things don't always work out the way we want them to on the schedule we want them to. Having a Plan B ensures that you can keep making progress, so eventually you can run the 26.2 miles, pass the bar or do whatever drives you.

## NOT NEGATIVE, BUT REALISTIC

**JANET:** You don't get what you want by thinking about it; you get what you want by working for it and having a plan to get it. Part of that is knowing the difference between being negative and being realistic. That's what having a Plan B is all about. Sometimes, no matter how much you want something to happen, it won't, and you've got to be ready to adjust.

For example, if you have terrible eyesight or you're 6'6" tall, you're not going to be a fighter pilot no matter how much you plan and how hard you dream. That's not negative thinking; it's realistic thinking. That's why it's important when you're making your plan to have someone in your life who can help you balance dreaming with being real.

Vince and I complement each other that way. He's the romantic and the dreamer. I swear, the reason we have a dimmer on every light switch in our house is so he can set the mood. I'm the hard-nosed realist, the one who says, "Great, but how do we get it done?" I go for the gut and don't sugarcoat anything. For us, it's a perfect balance. Vince reminds me what's possible, and I remind him what's probable.

**VINCE:** One of the most important steps you can take in staying positive is to quit comparing yourself to other people. Be the best you can be; let everyone else take care of themselves. When you compare yourself to everyone else, you're like the kid counting how many gifts the other kids got on Christmas morning; you're going to be disappointed.  Instead, make the most of what you have.  Be the best you can possibly be and no matter what happens in the end, you can't lose.

## END ZONE

**Things to think about & do after finishing this chapter**

■ Visualize your goals.
■ Take stock of your resources.
■ Identify the people you know will stick by you through all the ups and downs.
■ Write down your plan (see next page).

# WRITE YOUR PLAN:

## My long-term goal or dream:

_____

_____

_____

## The long-term steps I need to take:

1. _____

2. _____

3. _____

4. _____

## The medium-term steps I need to take:

1. _____

2. _____

3. _____

4. _____

## The short-term steps I need to take:

1. _____

2. _____

3. _____

4. _____

CHAPTER THREE

# FIND YOUR
# INVINCIBLE MOMENT

*"Life takes on meaning when you become
motivated, set goals and charge after them in
an unstoppable manner."*

— Les Brown

Some time ago I gave a speech for a huge pharmaceutical company.  I got up in front of the audience of executives, told some of my usual stories, got some laughs and did my motivational thing.  Then I asked them, "What opponents do you guys have?"  Now, this is one of the largest Big Pharma players in the world.  You wouldn't think they would have to worry about fears and doubts.  But you know what?  That's exactly what the people told me.  Internally and externally, these people fight against self-doubt, mental fatigue and fear every day.  Those are their opponents, and compared to them, competing pharmaceutical companies are a walk in the park.

One of the reasons that big corporations pay me to come in and deliver a good, rousing speech to their top brass is that even in the best organizations, attitudes can go sour from time to time.  Worry creeps in.  People start to get cynical.  Even the best begin to doubt themselves.  So I come in to remind them of what's possible for them.  They see me and say to themselves, "Yeah, Papale came from nowhere to make the Philadelphia-freaking-Eagles.  If he can do that, then I can handle my quarterly earnings reports!"

We all face doubts.  We all deal with opposition in our lives.  Sometimes the opponents come from outside us.  Rival companies want to take away our business.  Ex-spouses try to sabotage our personal lives.  Employers lay us off while prospective new employers won't even return our calls, a situation that's unfortunately familiar to millions of Americans these days.  But more often, our adversaries are inside us.  They are our self-doubts about what we can do, our fears that we're not good enough or don't really deserve the success we already have.  Sometimes, the obstacle is our own body that becomes afflicted with disease, or our mind that fractures into mental illness.

## JANET'S WORDS FOR WOMEN

*We women tend to over-think things, and that can get in the way
of invincibility.  Of course there is a time to plan.  But there's
also a time to stop planning and just get it done.  I'm a doer; I
like to slap down the tape, throw paint on the walls and clean up*

*later. Some women spend so much time prepping that they forget to paint. Don't get paralyzed by details. At Penn, I saw lots of women and men who read a lot about life but didn't live it; they were book smart but had no street smarts. Get your nails dirty. You'll learn an awful lot more about life and yourself than you ever did by planning.*

Sometimes we even find ourselves fighting against things that we've deliberately sought out—running that first marathon, for instance, and struggling against pain and exhaustion to keep going and make it across that finish line no matter how long it takes. Only human beings are brave and crazy enough to seek out suffering on purpose. As Pogo said, we have met the enemy and he is us.

In the end, it doesn't matter whether the enemy comes from outside or inside. What matters is that at some point, every one of us—including you—faces a moment of truth. In that moment, victory seems impossible. Hope? Forget about it. We're at the limit of our strength and courage and it's easier to give up than to keep fighting. But we don't. For some reason—passion, stubbornness or just plain stupidity, maybe—we soldier on. We don't quit. We pick ourselves up like Rocky and come out of our corner swinging. And we win. Amazingly, we win.

That's what I call an Invincible Moment, and there's not an adult alive who hasn't had one. You've had one. Now, it may not have been as dramatic as making the Philadelphia Eagles after a million-to-one shot open tryout. That doesn't matter at all. Each of us has his or her own Mount Everest. For you, physical challenges might be easy, but saving your marriage might have been the hardest thing you ever did. For someone else, relationships might be simple but finding the discipline to lose 75 pounds might have taken a Herculean force of will.

The specifics are not important. What's important is that at one time in your life, you found the strength and will and guts to get off the mat and triumph at something even when nobody else believed you could. For one brief, shining moment, you were invincible. Believe me, that's going to change your life.

## THE INVINCIBLE TEMPLATE

The importance of an Invincible Moment isn't that it makes you feel good about yourself looking back. It's that it gives you a template for overcoming obstacles today and tomorrow! If you can isolate what made you able to overcome the odds and do what even you might not have thought you could do, then you can apply that same source of strength to the challenges you face in a changing world.

Whenever your Invincible Moment was, whatever the circumstances were, you did something extraordinary. What did you call on to make that happen? What did you find in yourself to get past the fear and doubt and achieve victory on that occasion? That's what you need to identify, because odds are that's still in you. It may have been lying hidden all these years, but that doesn't mean it's gone. When you find it, you can start relying on it again.

I've put together a worksheet you can use to start figuring out what made you invincible:

**My Invincible Moment:** _____

_____

**When it was:** _____

_____

**The circumstances:** _____

_____

**The character or mental qualities I drew on to make it happen:**

**i.** _____

**ii.** _____

**iii.** _____

**How those same qualities could help me overcome the challenges I face today:** _____

_____

## WHY INVINCIBILITY MATTERS

This book is about handling changing times and coming out on top. But the thing about changing times is that you don't know which way they're going to change next. One day you've got a great job and you're living high on the hog with a big paycheck. The next, you're being furloughed and suddenly there's only a severance check between your family and foreclosure. Being invincible during such times means having tools in your toolbox that you can draw on when your life switches gears suddenly; after all, you can't always predict what's going to happen tomorrow! This book is about handling changing times, reaching your full potential, and coming out on top.

Imagine how much easier it would be to handle challenging times if you could draw on the qualities that gave you resilience or integrity when you needed them most. Instead of improvising when life's shakeups happen (or in football parlance, calling an audible), you have resources you can draw on that you know will help you not only cope but achieve the objectives you have in mind. There's a lot of confidence in knowing that deep within you, you have the ability to clear the barriers that life throws in front of you. You're not helpless. You don't have to make it up as you go along. You're in control. And even though you might be confused or scared to death, you can handle it. That's what being invincible is all about.

> ▶INVINCIBLE WISDOM
>
> *"It's not the load that breaks you down. It's the way you carry it."*
>
> — *Lou Holtz*

**JANET:** How can being invincible make a difference in life? Well, in your day-to-day routine, it might not. But eventually, a crisis is going to cross your path, and that's when invincibility means more than anything. Let's say that life hits you with a devastating surprise: your spouse informs you one day that he's been having an affair and wants a divorce. Your whole world is thrown into turmoil. Do you beg him to stay? Sign whatever legal papers he shoves in front of you? Vow revenge? Slip into a year-long depression that leaves your kids defenseless? Maybe…unless you have an Invincible Moment to draw on.

If you do, you think back to that time. Maybe it was when you faced down a bullying superior at your first post-college job; you'd had enough and though you risked getting fired, you knew you had to stand up for yourself. So you did. You found the self-control to say the right things and the fortitude not to back down, and you wound up not only getting the guy off your back, but you ended up with his job when he was fired a few months later!

Now, in the middle of your pain and feelings of betrayal, you draw on those same tools. You maintain control, say only what must be said, and save your grieving for a time when it doesn't impact your children. You come out the winner and you build a new life knowing that you kept things positive, didn't let your spouse drag you down to his level, and protected your kids. That's the power of knowing what made you invincible.

## WHEN I FOUND MY COURAGE

**VINCE:** I've had a few times when I found guts and determination that I didn't know I had, but the one that made the most impact on my later years came during my first tryout camp for the Eagles in 1976. When you're a totally untested rookie like I was, you can be cut at any time, and I was very aware of that fact. So when the team had a preseason road

*Nobody took me too seriously ... even security guards were laughing at me. The sweetest payback is getting The Last Laugh!*

game against the Miami Dolphins in August, and Coach Vermeil came and told me I would be starting and playing the entire first half of the game, I knew this was a chance to lock up my spot on the team.

Trouble was, I was a nervous wreck. I was also sporting a first-degree separation of the right shoulder and was still in a lot of pain. I thought I knew the playbook, but did I? I knew this was a turning point, possibly in my entire life, and the thought dumped about a ton of pressure on my shoulders. But I thought of the guys in Philly who were counting on me, looking ahead to what making the team could mean for me, figured I could take the pain in my shoulder for a lousy 30 minutes on the field, sucked it up and played my best. Coach started using my gung-ho style of play as an example for the entire team and of course, I would end up making the squad.

I had defied the incredible odds against a tryout player with no college experience making the roster of an NFL club. I'd done it with enthusiasm, passion, and a ridiculous amount of hard work and preparation. But in that moment, I'd also done it with perspective and the knowledge that I was strong enough to endure just about anything. Those qualities came in very handy when I was diagnosed with early stage colon cancer 25 years later. When I got that frightening diagnosis, I was in total shock, but was able to use my tools to beat the disease. I knew my body was strong because I'd worked hard to keep it that way. My sense of perspective told me that this wasn't the end of the world, just a speed bump. Thanks to Janet, I didn't panic, even if I wanted to. Yes, I felt sorry for myself and got depressed. But she helped me snap out of it and I did what was needed to be done and today I'm healthier than ever.

By the way, being invincible doesn't mean you'll be without fear, anger or a feeling of being a victim when life shocks the crap out of you. When they told me I had a cancerous polyp in my colon, I was scared to death! But being invincible is about getting past those feelings and doing what needs to be done. Sometimes, being a hero is about doing what must be done, quietly, without fanfare or complaining.

# INVINCIBLE MOMENT

Lu Ann Cahn is a broadcaster and Emmy winning journalist in my hometown of Philadelphia. She's also an amazing lady, something you'll see as she shares her Invincible Moment:

"I had just turned 35. My daughter was four years old. I'd just recovered from surgery to remove my large intestine because of ulcerative colitis. I was back at work as a TV news reporter when I started feeling a vague mass in my right breast. My doctor looked at my mammogram and said, 'Your mammogram is negative. You have no breast cancer in your family. I'm not concerned about it.'

"Six months went by while the lump kept growing. I started feeling it every night before I went to bed. Finally, one day in November 1990 there was a headline in the Philadelphia Inquirer: 'Young Women Dying of Breast Cancer with Negative Mammograms.' I went to a breast surgeon. It was probably a cyst, but I needed to be reassured.

"The surgeon felt the lump, was concerned, and aspirated some of it with a needle to perform a biopsy. The next day his office called asking me to come back. My husband and I sat in his office as he told me, 'You have a tumor that's malignant.' I had breast cancer.

"I thought it was a death sentence. This was 1990. There were no pink ribbon races and walks. There were few women who'd talked publicly about breast cancer. I felt alone with an aggressive breast cancer that had been allowed to grow for six months while I'd been reassured it was nothing. Inside I was screaming. I was furious. I was horrified. I was terrified I wouldn't survive to raise my sweet daughter.

"Then I knew what I would do. I would tell everyone, anyone. I would scream this story, write this story, tell this story everywhere and anywhere I could. I would document my treatment. I would expose myself because I had to let other women know. I had to tell them mammography isn't perfect especially for young women with dense breasts. Just because you're young doesn't mean you can't get breast cancer. Just because it's not in your family history doesn't mean you're safe. If your doctor won't check the lump you feel, find someone who will.

"I'd never felt so strong and so scared and so sure in my life. I did not know if I would survive. I did not know if anyone would listen to me. I only knew everything in my heart and soul compelled me to open my life and my diagnosis and treatment to my community.

"My breast cancer was fast growing but amazingly, I caught it before it spread. I had six months of chemotherapy. My hair fell out. I wore a wig. I had a mastectomy with reconstruction. I told my story in the spring of 1991. WCAU set up self-exam workshops and mammography clinics throughout our community. Our documentary 'Breast Cancer: My Personal Story' won numerous awards.

"I marched in Harrisburg for better mammography. I marched in Washington for more funding. I survived when so many other young breast cancer patients and friends who marched by my side didn't make it. I don't know why I survived and they didn't.

"What I do know is that I'm grateful for every day. To this day there are still women who come up to me and say 'I do breast self exams because of you,' or 'I felt a lump and was diagnosed early because I saw your story.' It fills my heart when I hear that and I know it's because I had an Invincible Moment—a moment when I knew that I could not be silent."

## REPLICATING YOUR INVINCIBLE MOMENT

Once you know what enabled you to have your Invincible Moment, you need to figure out how to tap the same qualities again and again, whenever you're facing a rough time or a change that sends you reeling. The goal is to replicate your Invincible Moment on command when you need it, so that no matter what happens, you have what it takes to rise above the circumstances and everyone's doubts and get the job done.

Think back on your Invincible Moment. Really relive it in all its detail, good and bad. Now think about all the doubts and obstacles you faced: the people who told you what you wanted to do was impossible, the voice in your head that said you didn't have what it took, the lack of money or time or talent. Next, what made the difference in you overcoming those fears and hurdles to be successful? Was it your work ethic? Discipline? Positive thinking? Great relationships? Integrity? What was the X factor that made you have an Invincible Moment?

Now bottle it. Remember it. Look at yourself today and find that same quality in yourself. It's still there, like I said. When I was diagnosed with cancer, I found the same passion for health and fitness that had enabled me to make the Eagles, and it has helped me not only beat cancer but become more fit and youthful than a lot of men half my age. (I'll share some of those secrets to my fitness later in this book.) I'll keep holding on to that passion and knowledge as part of my toolkit, and when life throws me another curveball, I'll be ready to pull it out if I need it.

You have that within you, too, right now. Finding that key to invincibility will put you in position not only to survive changing times, but thrive.

## END ZONE

**Things to think about & do after finishing this chapter**

■ Reflect on your personal Invincible Moment.

■ Make a list of the obstacles and barriers you faced and why.

_____

_____

_____

_____

_____

■ Write down what enabled you to rise above them and have an Invincible Moment.

_____

_____

_____

_____

_____

■ Ask other people who know you well what they think your most invincible qualities are. Do their answers match what you think?

_____

_____

_____

_____

_____

## END ZONE

- Choose up to three invincible qualities. These could be anything from your ability not to get stressed out to your knowledge of the law.

_____

_____

_____

- List areas of your life today—relationships, job situations, etc.— where you need to be invincible and how your invincible qualities could help.

_____

_____

_____

_____

_____

_____

# CHAPTER FOUR

# EVERYTHING STARTS
## WITH THE
# FUNDAMENTALS

*"First master the fundamentals."*

— Larry Bird

You know that play you see in NFL games sometimes where the wide receiver takes off like a bat out of hell without ever looking at the quarterback, the QB throws a bullet where he receiver will be, and at the last second the wideout turns his head, picks up the ball in the air and grabs it? That does not happen by accident. Teams rehearse that and all sorts of other plays at every practice. They are part of pro football's fundamentals.

Coach Vermeil was a teacher before he became a coach, and he never stopped teaching after he took over the Eagles. He was a stickler for the fundamentals. Before each practice he used to make sure that we had 30 minutes on the field just working on specific fundamental drills. One would be the "quick hands" drill: we would turn your back to someone throwing the football, he would fire the ball at your head, and at the last second he would shout, "Ball!" You had to turn and grab the ball before it smacked you in the face. All I can say is, thank God we were wearing helmets.

I also worked on the one-hand catch drill, the tap drill (where you catch a ball near the sidelines and work on keeping your feet in bounds even as the rest of your body is falling out of bounds), and others. The reason you see guys able to do those things during NFL games is that they have worked on them hundreds or even thousands of times in practice, over and over again, in the heat, wearing full pads, wishing they could be doing anything else.

The fundamentals are the basic, essential skills that you've got to master if you're going to have any success in your chosen field. They're repetitive, tiresome and they are definitely not flashy or sexy. They are also the bricks and mortar for everything that you do. You may hate them, you may not want to work on them, but if you're smart you'll devote at least some of every day to perfecting them.

## BUILDING BLOCKS

Now, I'll confess right now that I loved those fundamental drills. My posse, my entourage—otherwise known as the "project boys" I had grown up with who went into the stratosphere when I made the team— would come to practices to watch me go through drills. This was my time to bond with them. They would scream and yell when I did a tip drill successfully or didn't get a football in the kisser during quick hands; I would wave at them and grin and have a great time. It was a joy to practice on those days.

I also knew that the relentless practice was making me a better player. It was refining my hand-eye coordination, improving my balance, and sharpening my reaction time. Those would all come into play during the season and could make the difference between winning and losing at least once. I never resented working on the fundamentals the way that some guys did. Maybe it was because I didn't play college ball, so the endless drills weren't quite as old hat to me as to other players.

I've always made a point to learn the foundational skills of everything I have tried, from teaching to being a mortgage broker. The fundamentals are the building blocks that everything is based on. They are the basic moves, the boring but reliable tactics that make everything else possible:

- **In baseball:** Stepping toward the target when you throw, keeping your head down when you hit, etc.

- **In basketball:** Setting a good screen, watching the ball handler's midsection when you're on defense, and so on.

- **In sales:** Being an active listener, asking for the sale, etc.

- **In driving:** Keeping your hands at 10 and 2, checking your blind spots and so on.

Becoming proficient at the fundamentals makes it easier to climb to higher and higher levels of skill. Isn't getting better what it's all about?

## JANET'S WORDS FOR WOMEN

*Your fundamentals are your core values. When you lose yourself because of stress or disappointment, you can go back to those values and surround yourself with people who believe in you. It's a big, bad world and when you take risks, it's okay to fail and be afraid. But when you do, have the fundamentals in place: val-*

ues and people who love you unconditionally. Both are vital for women. It's equally important to recognize your patterns in life. When something goes wrong, is it because you made the same choice as the last time? Do you keep picking the wrong kind of man over and over? Women tend to be more introspective than men, but we also beat ourselves up more. Be kind to yourself, but look at the patterns honestly. If they're bad, change them.

## WHEN THINGS DON'T GO PERFECTLY

The trouble is, there's nothing about any of those things that's glamorous— and that's the problem. We live in an age that's obsessed with quick fame and instant success. Forget about paying dues; we want the movie deal, the endorsement deal, the big car and the reality show yesterday. Learn the fundamentals? That's for our grandparents. I see so many professional ath- letes today with poor fundamentals that it makes me sick. Pitchers who forget to cover first base, outfielders who can't hit the cutoff man, wide receivers with insane speed who don't work back to the ball. It's ridiculous. Everybody is so eager to get to the end zone that they don't want to run the first 90 yards.

What the seekers of easy success and fame don't get is that you really don't need the fundamentals...as long as everything goes perfectly. But just how often does that happen? I'll tell you: never. If you shortcut your way to the top based on luck and connections, the first time things go sour you'll fall all the way to the bottom because you have nothing to rely on. Working on the fundamentals gives you discipline, focus, and preci- sion and leads to gradual, well-earned improvement. When you have strong fundamentals, even when things crumble, you've got skills to fall back on so that you can regroup. Think about some of the reality TV stars and other "insta-celebrities" who didn't have that. As soon as they hit a few bumps, they were done. No character, no pride, no work ethic—no future.

But when things go bad, and you have sound fundamentals, it's incredible what you can do. One of the best examples I can think of came in a Major League Baseball playoff game between the New York Yankees

INVINCIBLE WISDOM

> INVINCIBLE WISDOM

*"The key to winning baseball games is pitching, fundamentals, and three run homers."*

— *Earl Weaver*

and the Oakland Athletics on October 14, 2001. If you're a baseball fan, you probably already know the one I mean. With a runner on base, an A's batter got a base hit and in trying to throw the runner out at home, the Yankees outfielder threw the ball at least 20 feet from the catcher. Total defensive breakdown and a run scored, right? Wrong. Derek Jeter, Yanks' shortstop and captain, had followed the fundamentals by backing up the cutoff man and he was lined up to grab the errant throw. He appeared out of nowhere, snatched the ball, and on the run flipped it to the catcher, who tagged the runner out. End of rally and end of series.

It was one of the best plays anyone had ever seen. It came from nothing more than observing the fundamentals, which put Jeter in the right place at the right time. To this day, it's known simply as "The Flip."

## COMING BACK TO THE BASICS

The value of fundamentals applies in every walk of life, from athletics and business to academia and family. In today's economic situation, when things are changing so fast, the fundamentals have never been more important. If you've lost your job, you're being forced to reinvent yourself so that you can make a comeback and support your family. That means getting back to some solid, timeless skills: interviewing well, writing a strong resume, remembering people's names when you meet them, being not just on time for meetings but early. Again, none of this is glamorous, but it's necessary. The boring stuff that you let slide when things are good can save your ass when things aren't so good.

Even if you still have your job, odds are the changing times have your employer emphasizing some old-fashioned fundamental values: conserving to save the company money, working longer hours, everybody pitching in to do each other's job and so on. That's what you do when you're tightening your belt and trying to survive, and if you can't or won't do the fundamentals, you might be cut loose.

**JANET:** The basics give you something in life to go back to when you're confused. If you build your career on a solid foundation of skills and routines, when you get off course you can go back to them until you get your bearings. We've all done that at one time or another. There's something incredibly comforting about those brick-and-mortar behaviors. They give you an anchor and they also give you peace of mind. You know that no matter what happens you're never helpless. You always have options.

## CROSSING OVER

**VINCE:** The great thing is that when you put in the time to master the fundamentals in one discipline, you do a lot more than become good at that set of skills. Let's say you're in marketing for a company. Your fundamentals might include knowing how to do market research, knowing how to write marketing copy with a call to action, and analyzing market data. Or maybe you're a graphic designer, in which case your fundamental skill set would include things like knowing how to use Photoshop, choose colors for four-color printing and lay out a magazine page. But when you spend years making those skills virtually automatic, are you just learning those skills and nothing else?

Of course not. The work crosses over from one skill to another. You're making the fundamentals a habit, a part of your basic makeup. For most people, I think investing the hours, sweat and tedium to get good at the basics also shows them how valuable that investment is. When you take the time to conquer the fundamentals in one area, you're probably going to apply that same lesson in others. The fundamentals become a way of life.

I know it's been that way for me. I enjoyed the blood, sweat and tears of practice when I was in the NFL, but I also learned how important it was to learn the fundamentals in anything. These days, I'm a professional speaker, but I prepare for each speech the way I prepared for a game back when I was playing football. The field is different but the approach is identical: repetition, follow a blueprint that works, and refine it until it's perfect. I do that with every speech I give.

## INVINCIBLE MOMENT

My good buddy and former NFL brother in arms Dennis Franks honors
us with his own Invincible Moment:

"In 1982 after leaving professional football, life was not so easy.
No more bright lights, no more Sunday afternoons at the Vet or
Silverdome, no more Monday Night Football games. The toughest plays
were ahead of me in the game of life, where the winner survived and
thrived and the loser was doomed to telling the stories of the good old days
and earning minimum wage. I had a college education, six years in the
NFL, and after six months out of the league I was jobless."

"I was sinking fast, in denial, drinking and partying way too much
with absolutely no direction.  Then a former teammate of mine from the
Detroit Lions, Dave Parkin, a Utah State graduate, visited with me. He
flat-out said, "What happened? You don't seem like the Denny Franks I
know. You look like you gained quite a bit of weight and you're sluggish
and unmotivated." He was right: I started my career at 255 pounds and
by the end I was tipping the scales at nearly 300 pounds. With a six-foot,
two-inch frame, I resembled a cinder block. Dave, in a strong and caring
voice, said, "Get your head out of your ass and get that energy back. You
need to be headed in a better direction."

"I had every excuse in the book: things have not been easy,
being a football player, and more, but he stopped me and said, "You are a
FORMER football player." That really sunk in, but what really made the
difference was that Dave said, "Let me help you." I decided to make a
change. Dave followed through with his offer and in six months my life
turned completely around. I lost 65 pounds and have kept the weight off.  I
started my own weight management business that has evolved into a product and an Internet marketing company.  I have had complete success
financially and now I'm helping others to do the same. It all came down to
someone reaching out…and me accepting the challenge to make a difference and be somebody."

## IT'S WHAT NO ONE SEES THAT MATTERS

Here's the hardest thing about the fundamentals: nobody sees or appreciates them. More to the point, people only notice them when you don't execute. After all, they aren't flashy. They're supposed to be routine. So you might feel unappreciated if you're great at the basics but nobody gives you credit for it. Trust me; don't be. The people who know your business know somebody who does the essential stuff well. Those might not be the people who get the headlines, but they are the people who stick around for the long term.

Excellence is invisible. It takes endless effort to make something look effortless. For proof, I give you Lady Gaga. I went to one of her concerts with my daughter (yes, I'm that hip) and Gabriella remarked how loosey-goosey Gaga was with the audience. I said, "Honey, that is all programmed. Do you know how hard she works and how many hours she puts in so she can look so casual and unrehearsed on stage? Do you have any idea what kind of condition she has to be in to do what she does for two hours?"

The same is true for the most incredible performer I've ever seen, Madonna. I saw her in concert a few years ago, running all over a 30 or 40-yard outdoor stage in the Philadelphia summer heat, not lip synching but singing live, not getting tired. That stuff does not happen by accident. It's

> **INVINCIBLE WISDOM**
>
> *"No matter what accomplishments you make, somebody helps you."*
>
> — *Wilma Rudolph*

the product of one hell of a lot of work, work that no one else but the people doing it will see or appreciate. But when you work that hard, you'll know it and you'll appreciate it.

I remember reading about Rod Stewart, one of my favorite singers. A few years back, he released an album of standards—you know, songs by Cole Porter, the Gershwins, people like that. He said that he used to sing all those songs while warming up before shows because they were challenging and took him through the vocal scale. Then someone heard him singing backstage and told him he should make an album of them, and that record was one of the most successful of his 30-year career. That's what can happen when you stick to the fundamentals and do them right, no matter who might be watching or listening.

## DO YOU NEED A COACH?

**JANET:** Of course, not everybody is good at the fundamentals. Some people just don't have the focus or discipline to get really good at them. That's when you should get help. For example, our daughter Gabriella was studying for her college board exams and while she gets As in school, her teacher told us that she lacked the kind of math fundamentals that would enable her to score well on a standardized test like the SAT. Well, in this house if you can't do something, you don't try to be a hero. You get a coach.

We hired a tutor to work with her on the fundamentals of the math she needed to do well on the college boards. It was a lot of hard work, but she did it and she had a great coach to help her. As we were finishing this book, Gabby retook the test and boosted her score by a whopping 250 points.

If you're making the same fundamental mistakes over and over, there's no shame in getting an independent, unbiased person to work with you and give you his or her opinions. In fact, the only shame is in not being smart enough to ask for help! Remember, just because something is easy for another person doesn't automatically mean it will come naturally for you. Stop comparing yourself to some nonexistent ideal, figure out what you have to get done, find someone to help you get better, and do the work. That's the process the great ones, no matter how talented they were, all had to go through. In fact, it's what made them great.

## END ZONE

**Things to think about & do after finishing this chapter**

■ Ask yourself what the fundamentals of your profession or vocation are.
■ How much time have you invested in mastering them?
■ Have you bypassed them because they seem boring or unnecessary? What have been your results?
■ Describe your ideal fundamentals-mastering regimen.

**Skills:** _____

_____

_____

**Routine to master them:** _____

_____

_____

**How much time you need:** _____

_____

_____

**How often you will practice:** _____

_____

_____

# CHAPTER FIVE

# WHAT ARE YOU FIGHTING FOR?

*"I am here for a purpose and that purpose is to grow into a mountain...I will apply ALL my efforts to become the highest mountain of all and I will strain my potential until it cries for mercy."*

— Og Mandino

One day after the DVD of Invincible came out in late 2006, a woman called me. She told me that her daughter was dying of cancer and that she had lost her job and given up on everything. But then she said to me, "I have to thank you. You've given me a reason to go forward and to go deeper within myself. I haven't really gotten as far down as I think I could. Everybody is relying on me, and I need to find a way to make this work. I don't want money. I just wanted to thank you."

I didn't know what to say. What do you say to that kind of pain and bravery? Later, she sent me an article that had been written about her sad story. I never did find out what happened to her or her daughter, but I hope that my story did a tiny bit to help them find courage and peace. In any case, it's a fantastic and poignant reminder of something I believe to be true for all of us:

## *If you're going to survive hard times and be your best, you need a reason.*

Why do you do what you do? Why do you get up in the morning and go to work? Why do you work two jobs, get up before sunrise to run ten miles or live on coupons so you can set aside some money for your kids' college education? If you're going to push yourself beyond normal limits or endure hardships, you need a reason for doing it. You need a purpose. You need to know what you're fighting for.

Some people that I talk to either have no reason or the wrong reasons. One of the wrong reasons to do something is money. Money isn't a reason; it's an outcome. Don't get me wrong, I like having money as much as the next guy. Too many people these days don't have enough of it, and that's terrifying. But money is just a tool, and it can ruin your life as easily as it can help it. If you're working or suffering just so you can bring home a lot of money, wake up. You're in prison and you need to break free.

Giving your kids a better life, helping people in your community, improving your health, raising money for an important cause—those are all reasons to take on extra work or beat yourself up in the gym. The simple truth is that even the most jaded and cynical among us need to be

> **INVINCIBLE WISDOM**
>
> *"When I chased after money, I never had enough. When I got my life on purpose and focused on giving of myself and everything that arrived into my life, then I was prosperous."*
>
> — *Wayne Dyer*

inspired. We can't just go on for years without some greater purpose behind what we do, or we wind up empty and dead inside. What happens when things change and your applecart turns upside down? When you have no "Why" behind the toil and sacrifice, you have nothing left to live for. That's a dark, dangerous place to be.

## MY REASON

JANET: I sometimes wonder if Vince would have made the Eagles if he had held anything back. He went into the whole experience balls-out and naked because he didn't know how to do it any other way. He let his passion be his reason, and that made him able to throw his body around recklessly and play with total abandon. I think that was the key to his success.

But as life changes, your reasons change. When you have kids, suddenly you're doing everything for them. They're the only people who matter, and not only does your purpose change but what you'll do to achieve it does, too. Vince was able to do what he did because it came at a perfect time in his life when he was in a bubble of solitary machismo. He could be self-indulgent and chase his dream, so he did.

VINCE: Janet's right, but later on, when I made the team, I found a new reason to keep throwing my body into 280-pound guys like a pinball: the guys I grew up with. See, I may not have wanted to be overly famous because of making the team, because I didn't want my teammates to resent me—but that doesn't mean I didn't know exactly what my fame might mean to the blue-collar folks in Philly.

1976 was a rough year. Unemployment was high. Vietnam had just ended badly. The city needed a hero, and I knew that even though I didn't think I was the best guy for the job, once I made the team I would be that hero. I didn't want to let down the city that I loved or the people who were like family.

So each weekend, I was fighting for the regular guys and gals in the cheap seats, the "nose bleeds' as we called them. I would hustle and sprint and throw my body around like I had a spare one in the locker room, and they would scream my name and whoop and holler. I think I gave them hope. Here I was, a local boy coming from nowhere to play for the team every kid in the city had dreamed about playing for! Damned right I would play like a maniac. I wasn't about to let my people down. My love of the game and my love of the fans probably kept me going for those three-plus years more than any- thing else.

## JANET'S WORDS FOR WOMEN

*We're caretakers, aren't we ladies? We take care of everybody but ourselves. It's so easy to keep busy doing things for other people that you never really look at yourself. Your reason becomes taking care of everyone else, so when they are finally gone—when the kids go off to college, for example—you have no reason left. You don't know who you are. Women can spend a lot of time just keeping our feet but never going forward. But at some point, you have to figure out where you're going. You have to become your own reason; take care of yourself before you take care of anyone else. Nobody should be your whole life but YOU. It's not easy, but it can be done. Keeping yourself strong and growing is the only way to keep your relationships strong and growing, too.*

## YOU'RE EITHER FIGHTING FOR SOMETHING...

...or you're fighting against something. That's what I've found to be true. That's the choice each of us has to make during changing times. Do we find a new reason to keep fighting, maybe a new purpose in life? Or do we try to resist the change and hold on to what we already have? It's a tough choice and I can't say which is better for you. I do know that I look for inspiration. For you, inspiration might come in finding a new cause, like a new career or your own business. Or you might get motivated by defending the ground you're already standing on.

The point is, we all need a reason to keep battling. Sometimes, it doesn't make sense to fight against something that can't be stopped. It's like resisting the tide; you're going to lose no matter what. If your industry is changing like the dotcom world did back during the crash in 2000, continuing to insist everything is fine makes you look like Don Quixote, tilting at windmills. Then again, if you're fighting against the influence of negative people (the "bucket of crabs" that we'll talk about in a later chapter), that's to your benefit. It's less about for or against than about having a purpose and a reason to put out the effort, keep getting up when you fall down, and continue to give your goal everything you have.

If you don't find something to fight for or against, then it's easy to live aimlessly and wind up in places you didn't expect with a life you didn't really intend. You're either going somewhere on purpose or you're being carried by events and people beyond your control. When you're not fighting for a purpose, it's easy to become disengaged and let yourself go on autopilot. That's how you wake up one day and find you've wasted ten years that you'll never get back, and maybe some of the dreams you had are gone, too.

## INVINCIBLE MOMENT

*Kim Dearman (then Kimberly Castle) was a Hattiesburg, Mississippi-based attorney who closed loans for clients who used the now-defunct Countrywide Home Loans. Like so many others in the mortgage industry during the overheated real estate boom, she simply provided the title and closed the loans as fast as she could to keep up with demand. She didn't underwrite them nor review the information provided to the mortgage company. Yet when everything fell apart and it became clear that Countrywide had been part of a massive fraud, CEO Angelo Mozilo escaped prosecution while Dearman* and several others took the fall.

After pleading not guilty and going to trial, in 2007 she was sentenced to consecutive 48-month sentences and ordered to pay $1.3 million in restitution—an outcome she insists is consistent with the government's desire to find scapegoats while sparing the power players. "We argued in court that I was just a closing attorney and that these things were common practice at Counrtywide," she told The Conference Board Review for a spring 2011 article. "They didn't want Countrywide," Dearman said. "That was obvious. And it was very odd, because we were providing them—even in court at trial—with direct evidence of the crimes committed as standard practice within Countrywide. But the government just sat there. They didn't want to hear it. They just wanted me."

Dearman spent three-and-a-half years in prison, was disbarred, faced negative press coverage when she was released and tried to seek employment, and must pay $1,500 a month to compensate for a crime that she did not commit. Despite this, she insists that trial and prison were actually beneficial to her. "I came out better than before I went in, thanks to God," she says. "I lost it all and I thought I would lose my mind, because no one would listen and the injustice was just too much. But I overcame and I have gained back the ground taken from me. I have my job back, my life back and I am working with others to help get their lives back.

"I didn't know that I could make it," Dearman continues. "There were days in the beginning when I thought I would die, but I refused to let the government have the last say. I have the last say and I will live a more abundant life no matter what they try to do to me."

## A TIME OF QUESTIONING

**JANET:** This is a period in our country unlike any we've seen since the Great Depression. During this time, people are starting to question what they believe. They're fighting to keep their houses and families. People are losing everything, and

▶ INVINCIBLE WISDOM

*"The purpose of life is a life of purpose."*

— *Robert Byrne*

they don't know what to believe in. We know people whose lives have been turned upside down and their relationships are suffering as well. There's stress, conflict and a lot of desperation.

When you're trapped in a terrible situation, it can be hard to keep going if you don't have the sense that you're doing it for a bigger purpose. Vince and I know a man who has been out of work for two years, a situation that would crush anybody's spirit. But somehow, this guy keeps applying for jobs and going on interviews. He hasn't given up. Why? Because he wants to take care of his family. That's his reason.

**VINCE:** I think most of us already have powerful reasons in our lives, but we're too busy or distracted to see them that way. You've got to choose your reason. You've got to question everything that's come before and get out of your comfort zone with your reason, so that it doesn't fit in with your old beliefs. If the recession destroyed your belief that you could be happy working only for material gain, then your new reason had better be about more than money. Otherwise you're just running in place and not honoring the person you're becoming.

## FIND WHAT MATTERS TO YOU

How do you find your reason? I think it's as simple as asking two questions:

1. *What do I care about most?*

2. *How can what I do serve what I care about?*

*My inspiration, a Wounded Warrior, the protector and keeper of our dreams.*

If you can't answer the second question—or if the answer is, "It can't," then you might need to ask a third, tougher question: "Do I need to change my path in order to serve what's important to me?" That might not be an option, but I think it's worth asking the question. Like Janet said earlier, a big part of finding that reason and purpose is simply looking at the things in our lives in a different way.

If that doesn't work for you, I recommend finding a way to get some perspective. For example, this book is dedicated to the Paralyzed Veterans Association, a group I've worked with for a long time. The PVA does vocational training for veterans who've lost limbs or been paralyzed so they can get jobs. I wasn't in the military, so why do I work with them? Because these men and women deserve every bit of our respect. They gave part of their bodies to protect our freedoms and safeguard the American Dream, and that sacrifice should be honored. So I go and visit the vets whenever I can. It always humbles and inspires me. I've seen men and women who've had arms and legs blown off. On one

53

trip, a triple amputee put his arm around me, sobbing, and told me that I was an inspiration to him.

*I was an inspiration to* him?

When you see something like that, you find a strong reason really quick. One disabled vet told me, "Our dreams weren't shattered. We just have to reprogram them so they're attainable with the cards we've been dealt." These people are fighting for self-respect, acceptance and dignity. All they ask for is a second chance and it is our duty to give them that. They find a reason to face the world each day with their mangled bodies and their wheelchairs and their prosthetics and keep going...and by God, if they can do that, I can make them a reason why I do what I do.

If you're not fighting for something good and honest and precious in this world, then there's no point. Whatever you have to do to find your reason, do it. You'll never regret it.

## END ZONE

**Things to think about & do after finishing this chapter**

■ Write down what you do professionally or how you spend most of your time.

_____

_____

_____

_____

■ Write down what is most important to you: your kids, the environment, etc.

_____

_____

_____

_____

■ How does the first serve the second?

_____

_____

_____

_____

■ If it doesn't, what needs to change so that you have a reason to do what you do and keep doing it?

_____

_____

_____

_____

# CHAPTER SIX

# NOBODY EVER DROWNED IN SWEAT

*"Dictionary is the only place that success comes before work. Hard work is the price we must pay for success."*

— Vince Lombardi

When Dick Vermeil took over as head coach of the Philadelphia Eagles, the locker room and other team areas quickly became filled with signs displaying his favorite motivational sayings. One of my favorites and the one that sums up his attitude toward preparation for the game of football is, "Nobody ever drowned in sweat."

It doesn't take a lot of thinking to figure out the message. Hard work never killed anyone. Hard, relentless, exhaustive work was the cornerstone of Coach's method of preparing his teams to win, or at least to compete. Remember, when he took over the team, the Eagles were barely competitive. A once-proud franchise was in shambles and fan support and confidence were wavering. That presents someone trying to improve the team with many problems. First, attendance tends to drop, which means lower revenues. With less money, you can't sign many of the players you covet, can't upgrade facilities and so on. Also, when a team is terrible, free agents usually don't want to sign contracts. Everybody wants to join a winner.

That means that you're stuck rebuilding with your existing roster plus other players who are hungry for jobs. Coach Vermeil knew that at least at first, we weren't going to be able to compete with other teams on the basis of talent. We didn't have it. But he was determined that we would surpass them in the areas we could control: fitness and conditioning, preparation, strategy and out-and-out effort. But to build that kind of a team, Coach needed to weed out the guys who weren't willing to bleed and give every last bit of effort they had. So he designed his first training camp to separate the hungry, dedicated players from the ones just looking for a paycheck.

When I showed up for camp, I saw the "Nobody ever drowned in sweat" sign outside the locker room at Widener University. We started camp on July 3; remember, it was the bicentennial year. The next day, jets were flying over the stadium, but Vermeil was so focused on the camp that he kept wondering why all those planes were in the air. Finally someone said, "Dick, it's the Fourth of July." That's how intense the atmosphere was. It was work, work and more work, and if you couldn't take it, you went home.

# He Can Kill Us, But He Can't Eat Us

Camp was so merciless that it might have been "illegal" in some states. Most pro training camps, the players would spend most of the time running plays and drills in light pads or no pads, which is cooler. But not Vermeil. To him, if you weren't in full pads, you really weren't working. Well, full pads are hot and heavy, and in July and August they might as well weigh about a thousand pounds. We were always in full pads and helmets. We'd practice at what's called a "thud tempo": you would hit guys at full speed above the waist only and wrap them up. To prevent injuries, there was no tackling and no hitting below the waist. It didn't matter, in full pads in the summer heat, it was pure hell.

Guys were falling over left and right from the heat and exhaustion. Coach's philosophy was that if you needed to take your helmet off, you could walk off the field and just keep walking. All-Pro tackle Stan Walters famously asked him, "Are you trying to kill the first 45 players to find the last five?" He wasn't trying to hurt us, of course. He was trying to see who wanted it the most. His thinking was that the guys who endured eight weeks of that torture would be the best conditioned, most disciplined, most passionate players in the league. They would be ready to endure any heat, cold or fatigue to win because they'd already done it in camp! Coach Vermeil put a lot of pressure on himself and his assistants during this time. As hard as we were working, they were working even harder.

The survivors started to say to each other, "He can kill us, but he can't eat us." When training was over for the day, we had to walk a half a mile up the street from the fieldhouse to the clubhouse. We called it the Bataan Death March. We weren't allowed to drive our cars to practice, though sometimes fans would drive down and take us to the clubhouse. You've never seen anyone more grateful than an Eagles player after a Vermeil practice getting into an air-conditioned automobile. Sometimes kids would come down and carry our helmets for us; one of my "helmet boys" is now the PA announcer for the Philadelphia 76ers, Matt Cord. We'd give the kids tape or whatever we had on us, and they loved it. I would go into training camp at 198 pounds and come out at 180. I would lose six to eight pounds in water weight in a single day. We'd all go to this place called the Campus Casino and drink beer right out of the pitcher.

Then we'd go to the special teams meetings a little light headed. The thing is, as punishing as those training camps were, they made us better. The players who survived and made the team had a feeling of camaraderie, because we knew we'd endured something that most people couldn't. We knew we were fit-

ter and tougher than any other NFL team. Personally, that 1976 camp made me work out even harder in the subsequent off-seasons so I could come to camp in peak shape and have a slightly easier experience. Even though we didn't win a lot of games those first couple of seasons, there was a lot of pride. We knew we had put in the work and were giving it everything we had, and eventually it would pay off.

## JUST ONE MORE

**JANET:** I was always known as the "one more" girl, because in gymnastics I was always the one saying, "Can't we do just one more?" I knew enough to value the chance to work hard, because getting that chance was not easy. As a child I had rheumatic fever and later a heart murmur. My parents were so worried about my heart that they wouldn't let me walk up steps; I had to take them sitting down. When I finally convinced my parents to let me try gymnastics, I was a joke. I was incredibly stiff. My uncle used to pay me 25 cents to make him laugh by doing my gymnastics routines. My mother would stretch me every night that I would cry out because it hurt so much. She would stop, but I'd say, "No, keep going! This is what I want."

I was one of nine kids, seven of whom were girls, all gymnasts. We were always competing with one another. We were all working hard, but I made sure I always worked harder because I wasn't as naturally talented as my sisters. We worked hard every day in our lives. If you wanted to go out, you cleaned your room. You learned to budget your time well so you had time to train. You learned to juggle and be efficient.

Everything I did was a crapshoot. Because I had lost my spleen and had no immune system, nobody wanted to take a risk on me athletically. I went from that situation to nearly making the Olympics, held back only by my knee injury. Hard work is what made that transformation possible.

## JANET'S WORDS FOR WOMEN

*Hard work is second nature to women who want to have it all, because trying to be a mom, a spouse and a professional is tough. I think that if you're going to work that hard, you need to love the situation you're in. Know what you want and just as important, what you don't want. Don't settle for less, because if you aren't happy, you won't want to put in the effort and you'll resent the people who are depending on you.*

## THE ENTITLEMENT VIRUS

**VINCE:** Janet's hardworking spirit has unfortunately become the exception, not the rule. Things have changed in our country. There's a disease running rampant and it's called entitlement. A lot of people don't know what it's like to pay the price for what they want, because it's been given to them. They don't understand what it means to put in sweat equity. Now, that may be changing because of the economic downturn we're still experiencing. I suspect that with a lot of wealth vanishing in the wind, there will be a lot fewer parents paying for their kids' college educations and a lot fewer new cars turning up in driveways for 18th birthdays or graduation gifts. I think that's a good thing.

The prevailing attitude out there, especially among the younger generation, seems to be that sucking it up, working hard and not quitting is not the way to succeed anymore. Now, we take short cuts. That's the kind of thinking that led to Wall Street meltdowns and banking failures in 2008 and gave us the Great Recession. I think there are three responsible parties in spreading the Entitlement Virus:

1. **Government** — Government—There are a lot of people getting money for doing nothing. Car companies and banks get bailed out when they're at risk of failure. Farmers get paid not to grow crops. Single mothers get paid not to work. Programs exist that out there that teach younger people to expect a bailout— or a handout. Why work when Uncle Sam is going to come to the rescue?

2. **Society** — Time was you had to work for years to master your craft and maybe become famous. Now, in the era of the Internet, all you have to do get on Letterman or pitch your own reality show. It's an age of instant pseudo-celebrity, and that's convinced a lot of young people that work is for suckers. Just write a blog about stupid stuff your father says, publish a book about it and wait for somebody to offer you your own television show. In my opinion, all of this cheapens the hard work required for real, lasting fame and success.

3. **Parents** — We all want what's best for our kids. But sometimes, what's best for our kids is to struggle. No child ever died from having to stay up all night finishing a science project that they left until the last minute. No high school senior ever went on a shooting spree because she had to work a part-time job to buy her own prom dress. But we live in the time of "helicopter parents" who don't want their offspring to suffer, and I think that makes kids weak and soft. Now don't get me wrong; I wouldn't subject my kids to some of the things that happened to me as a kid. I grew up in a period of postwar poverty, a rough time when the strap was most parents' response to a childrearing problem. I'm glad we've moved beyond that, but now I think we've gone too far.

If you want to thrive and be invincible during changing times, and reach your full potential, you had better be prepared to work harder than you have ever worked in your whole life. The workforce right now is flooded with former corporate executives, sales- people, lawyers, teachers and other professionals who thought they had locked up lucrative careers. Then...surprise! Now they're taking jobs out of their field at half pay and working longer hours than ever, and they're grateful to be working at all. Sometimes, being invincible means riding out the tough times as best you can until opportunity knocks. The only way to do that is to work your butt off.

## INVINCIBLE MOMENT

*Spiritual teacher Matthew Joyce shares an extraordinary Invincible Moment from when he was just a kid:*

*"When I was 11 years old I was skiing with a schoolmate. We came across a man in the snow with lots of blood everywhere. Three adults stood around the man in shock, doing nothing while he was bleeding to death. My friend and I asked what happened and learned he had taken a jump and impaled himself when he landed on the sharp end of his ski pole.*

*"Being Boy Scouts we set to work immediately. We sent one adult down to the lodge to get the Ski Patrol, one to block the jump so no one landed on the man, and the third to hike up the hill to direct the Ski Patrol. Then we treated the man for shock and applied pressure to stop the bleeding. All the while the adults were telling us what couldn't be done. But we had our first aid merit badges, we were boy scouts, and we were prepared. We didn't listen because we felt invincible.*

*"We ended up saving the man's life. He'd punctured his femoral artery and if not for our immediate actions would have bled to death before the Ski Patrol arrived. We later received commendation from the ski patrol, from the Boy Scouts, and were written up in the newspaper. It was a long time ago, but it changed my mindset about what is possible."*

## QUITTING ISN'T AN OPTION

Hard work isn't fancy. It's not sophisticated. But it works. There's no leveler like being willing to put in more effort than the other guy. Whatever changes come your way, if you are willing to work until you drop and never, ever quit, then you will give yourself the best chance of coming out ahead.

If you do it often enough, quitting becomes a habit. It becomes easier and easier to give up because you've done it before and it didn't kill you. That's not true. Giving up doesn't kill you right away; it's not the quick death of a heart attack, but that doesn't make it any less deadly. Over time, it eats away at your opportunities and your self-esteem. I think many of the people who will turn out to be part of your Bucket of Crabs (see chapter 17), the folks who resent your success and want to hold you back, do so because your hard work reminds them of the times they gave up. They know that there's nothing sweeter than success earned through sweat and determination, and nothing more bitter than success missed because you weren't willing to pay the price.

Sometimes, professional opportunity doesn't knock. You have to beat the door down until your hands are bloody, and only then do good things start to happen. Take the example of the book *Chicken Soup for the Soul*. You've heard of it, right? Jack Canfield and Mark Victor Hansen produced more than 200 books with that brand, created licensed properties worth over $1 billion, and moved more than 110 million copies before they sold most of their share in the brand in 2008. But that almost didn't happen. When they conceived of the idea of books containing other people's uplifting stories set around a central theme, no publisher wanted it. Jack and Mark spent years pitching the book to more than 130 publishers until finally, Health Publications picked it up for a pittance...and publishing history was made.

How long could you endure endless rejection and failure like that? Would it make it easier to know that success lay at the end of a string of people saying "No"? That's how it works. Gandhi said, "First they laugh at you, then they ignore you, then you win." That's a recipe for achievement—IF you're willing to keep pushing past the laughter and the people who won't give you the time of day.

> ### INVINCIBLE WISDOM
> *"The triumph can't be had without the struggle."*
>
> — *Wilma Rudolph*

## THE BEAUTY OF OBSTACLES

Am I suggesting you should work harder than you have to just because work is somehow noble? Of course not. If you can get what you want without having to work three jobs, do it. But it's true that hard work does breed habits that carry over into other areas of life: discipline, focus, attention to detail and stamina. I wouldn't have been half the player that I was in my short career if I hadn't worked so hard to be in great shape and make the most of my speed.

However, I think people are at their best when they're battling some obstacles. We weren't meant to be comfortable. We're strivers, climbers, and rebels. When we become complacent, we start to die. One piece of advice I would give is this: don't shy away from challenges, hard work or barriers when they come along. If there's something you really want, but a hell of a lot of sweat and hard work lies between you and it, embrace the work. You'll come out on the other side stronger and wiser. You'll feel great about yourself because you'll know you earned your success.

The other thing is, prepare to work hard when the need arises. If a job opportunity comes up, have your tools ready, grab them and jump in with all the effort you can muster. You'll be surprised how far that will take you. Some of the tools I recommend you keep on hand:

- **Show up early.** Getting a head start on the other guys always makes you look good and gives you time to make some of your mistakes before anybody is paying attention.

- **Find allies.** Some people are going to think you're showing them up by working so hard, so if you can find a few buddies who are willing to push as hard as you do. There's safety in numbers.

- **Plan your time.** When you have a long list of work to do, you need to use every second. Plan out how you'll use every hour and stick to your plan if at all possible.

- **Minimize distractions.** When you need to crank out work on deadline or need to focus on tiny details, find ways to keep other things out of your field of view. Shut off email, put on headphones, whatever it takes.

- **Distract yourself.** Wait, aren't I contradicting myself? Not really. There are times when you want to distract yourself from tedious or tiring work. Why do you think so many people listen to audio books on their iPods when they run? Come up with ways to occupy your mind elsewhere if you have to push through

Most of all, don't quit. Ever. Remember, winners never quit and quitters never win.

## END ZONE

**Things to think about & do after finishing this chapter**

■ Recall the times you worked harder than you thought you could. What enabled you to do it?

_____

_____

_____

_____

■ Go over your hard work toolkit and do an inventory of the tools you have in place.

_____

_____

_____

_____

■ Write down opportunities that exist in your life right now. With which ones would hard work give you the edge you need?

_____

_____

_____

_____

■ Who are the hardest working people you know? Ask them how they get motivated and keep from quitting when things get rough.

_____

_____

_____

_____

# CHAPTER SEVEN

# FIND A MENTOR

"I had for a friend a man of immense and patient wisdom and a gentle but unyielding fortitude. I think that if I was not destroyed at this time by the sense of hopelessness which these gigantic labors has awakened in me, it was largely because of the courage and patience of this man. I did not give in because he would not let me give in."

— Thomas Wolfe

In seventh grade I was introverted, insecure, withdrawn, undersized, confused and angry. Pimples were just starting to come. I was just plain awkward (wise guys who know me are probably saying, "Yeah, Papale, what's changed?"). With my father working long hours at Westinghouse (or on strike) and my mother falling deeper and deeper into mental illness, I didn't have anybody to talk to or to help me figure out how to be a man. I needed a mentor and I found one in my seventh grade phys-ed teacher and coach, George Corner.

George became the track coach at my school and later became football coach at my high school. When he did, he basically turned my life in the right direction. I had always been confident as an athlete, but that was mostly based on raw ability; I was always the fastest player on the field in whatever sport I played. But I was insecure about me, the person. I was ashamed of my mother's condition, stung by my father's lack of praise, and basically had no idea what I was going to do after high school.

Thanks to George's patient mentoring and advice, I learned to become a slightly more polished football player (though I would find out how raw I really was when I finally hit the pros) and a much more confident person. It was from him that I picked up a love of teaching, because I saw how much he loved his work and how much of a difference his attention made to the kids he worked with, mostly working-class guys like I was. If I had to choose one reason why I'm where I am today—an ex-NFL player and team captain, a speaker and author who's had an honest-to-God Hollywood movie made about his life—it would be the love and wisdom of George Corner.

**JANET:** I had my own version of George Corner, my gymnastics coaches Ginny and Bill Coco. They were my mentors when I was coming up. They taught me about life—how to live and how to travel, not just to go to a place for a competition and then leave. There are so many kids doing sports who travel but then forget about experiencing the world. It's not just about winning and losing; it's also about learning something about where you are and taking something away from each experience.

There's always someone wiser than you, always someone worth

listening to. Ginny and Bill taught me about travel, and I took that into my coaching at Penn. I always took my girls out and did things. I made sure they took the time to smell the roses. I became their mentor and I passed that lesson on to them. Hopefully, some of them will remember and pass it on to others. That's how mentors can impact not only the people they teach but others as well.

## JANET'S WORDS FOR WOMEN

*Women need to help each other. We have so much to offer, but too often we see each other as rivals. Women who've managed to have it all need to reach women and girls and let them know they don't have to limit themselves to being mommies. They can be career women, too, and mothers, and wives. Whatever they choose, they can be. It's important that women hear that from other women.*

## NOBODY MAKES IT ALONE

**VINCE:** Without mentors, Janet and I couldn't have made it this far. For me, Dick Vermeil was a mentor in his tough, understated way. Harold Carmichael, who took me to buy my first decent suit after I got my signing bonus, was a mentor. Denny Franks, who taught me that if the guy lined up opposite me on the line of scrimmage had white knuckles, he was charging, was a mentor. There have been many others. I owe a lot to a long list of great people.

So do you. If you've enjoyed any success in your life, your mentor is probably the person, after your parent or spouse, who's most responsible for helping you get there. A mentor tends to be even more influential in some ways than a parent, because he or she doesn't have a vested interest in your success. A parent might want you to do well to make him look good; a mentor doesn't care about that. Mentors are teachers, taskmasters and imparters of wisdom. A mentor will push you harder than you will push yourself and demand more of you than you thought you could give. You might hate him or her for it at the time, but you'll look back and be thankful. It's a mentor's job to bring out the best in us, even if we don't realize at the time that's what we want.

Someday, I want to write a book called, You Are What You Were When…, because what we are today begins and takes shape when we're in middle school, high school and college. That's when we can be molded and shaped. It's when experienced adults still tower over us like gods and we can learn more than we'll pick up in any classroom, if we'll only listen. Those early years determine so much about what we become as adults that I pity people who never had good mentors. When you are trying to survive changing times and come out of them smarter and more prosperous than before, you need a mentor by your side to guide you.

A mentor can be anyone: a coach, a teacher, a pastor, an uncle, an older sibling, even a boss. What they have in common is that a great mentor has been around the block. Mentors have seen it all and have a clearer perspective than you on what you're trying to achieve and what it's going to take to get there. A mentor doesn't get worked up over early successes or failures, because he or she knows that the game isn't won or lost in the first inning or in the first quarter. Mentors keep you calm, keep you focused, and kick your ass when you need it. They inspire you to want to do more and be more.

Does that sound like anyone who influenced you when you were younger? Who was your most important mentor?

## YOUR MENTOR IS THE CAPTAIN OF YOUR TEAM

I've talked about the importance of building a team of good people around you when you're trying to manage in challenging, changing times. Well, your mentor is the captain of that team. You might think it would be your spouse, but no. Your spouse loves you (presumably) and probably can't be counted on to be hard on you when you need it. But a mentor doesn't have to see you over the breakfast table in the morning. He or she can get in your face, call you on laziness or poor choices, and piss you

69

off for your own good without worrying about the consequences. That's why your mentor is captain!

Sometimes, your mentor will be the only member of your team. That was the case when I was a kid and coach Corner was there for me. I didn't really have anyone else, and that's when a good mentor becomes so incredibly important. When you're at a turning point, you need someone with a firm hand who's learned things the hard way—by making mistakes and paying for them.

**JANET:** You're never too old to learn. You always need someone to bounce ideas off of. Mentoring is about benefiting from someone else's experiences and wisdom. When you listen to people who are willing to share, you're not always reinventing the wheel. A mentor can tell you things that get you halfway to where you want to be. You don't have to make all the same mistakes and start from scratch. You can try new things and make new mistakes! Plus, when you doubt yourself, your mentor can help you reflect back on the trials and tribulations you've endured and realize that you have what it takes to overcome anything.

**VINCE:** A real mentor also empathizes with you and understands what you want. Not everyone responds to a swift kick in the backside. Some people need constructive criticism and positive coaching. Well, a good mentor will give you what you need; it's never about him or her. He or she will guide you, give you advice, and do what's best for you even if you don't understand it at the time. It's got to be someone you trust; you've got to have confidence that they have your best interests at heart.

Sometimes (actually, most of the time), mentors come into your life by accident. I think one of the best examples of this appears in the bestseller Tuesdays With Morrie. In it, Mitch Albom, a cynical columnist for the Detroit Free Press, visits his former sociology professor Morrie Schwartz every Tuesday for 14 weeks when he learns that Morrie is dying of Lou Gehrig's Disease. But the sessions quickly turn into lessons in which Morrie imparts a great deal of wisdom to the younger man, changing Albom's character in the process. If you haven't read this touching, moving book, I defy you to do it and not cry at the end.

# INVINCIBLE MOMENT

*Professional baseball scout Claudio Reilsono shares his Invincible Moment:*

"It was August 19, 1973. My uncle worked at Three Rivers Stadium, and he was taking me to my first Pittsburgh Pirates game. As soon as I walked in that place, the smells and the pictures of all the former Pirates and Steelers just mesmerized me. We went to the locker rooms and saw these big guys laughing and just having a good time. Then we walked up a ramp to get on to the baseball field and it was as if harps were playing. I was in awe of how big the place was, how green the field was. I knew what I wanted to do with the rest of my life: be in professional baseball.

"When I told my parents, my dad, Olindo, put his arm on my shoulder and said, 'If that is what you want to do, then I will do everything I can do make sure you have every chance to make that dream come true.' My mom Ida said, 'As long as you don't get hurt, and keep up your studies, I will always be by your side.' But I never expected other people to be so negative or just plain old rotten about my dream. Family members would say things like, 'Time to grow up, quit baseball and be a man,' and 'Get a real job,' or 'Be realistic.'

"It got worse when my mother passed away from cancer in October of 1988. I was devastated. On the first day of the viewing, I was walking towards the casket. A relative stopped me and said, 'Now it's really time to grow up, quit baseball and be a man!' What a terrible thing to say. My Dad put his arm around me and said, 'I know what you are thinking. You want to quit baseball. Claud, you are the only thing left to keep her dream and name alive. Don't stop.'

"I said to myself and my Mom, 'I won't quit! I am going to make it!' It took 13 years, five coaching jobs, hundreds of letters of rejection and unanswered calls. I coached at a small high school for $800 a year. I put up with abuse from jealous people who wanted to see me fail. Finally, I *could put that three-letter word "pro" by my name. I was hired by James L. Gamble, owner of the Global Scouting Bureau, in 2001 to become a professional baseball scout. Now I am with the Paramount Scouting Bureau as the Director of Professional Baseball Scouting and lead scout. I am the head baseball coach at Carnegie Mellon University. I'm a frequent TV and radio guest on stations all across the country. I teach baseball at clinics and camps, am a pro hitting instructor, have produced my own hitting video, and write for two sports magazines in Pittsburgh. I even announce boxing matches as well as being a co-host of a TV boxing show. I've built the life no one thought I could or wanted me to have...except my parents.*

*"I had people who tried hard to make the road tougher, but that did not stop me. Let nothing get in your way. As my Mom would tell me before every game, 'Show them your courage!'"*

## WHAT MAKES A GREAT MENTOR?

When you boil it all down, being a mentor is about giving the gift of your knowledge, experience, understanding and foresight to someone younger, without ever expecting a thing in return. Maybe that's what gives mentoring such power.

Coach Vermeil was a mentor for me, but in subtle ways. He wasn't a rah-rah motivator for me, but he taught me about the fundamentals—not just of football but of self and life. He was a mentor for me in his open-mindedness; he refused to do things the way every other coach did them, but found his own way and made it work. I trusted him because we came from the same place: he had an Italian-American background with a dad, Jean Louis, who was an auto racing pioneer. I knew that we shared many of the same values: passion, preparation, and hard work. He told me that those values came into play when he made the decision to put me on the roster in 1976. He was a character coach.

Dick was notorious for his endless workdays in preparing for the season; one of the reasons his players were willing to kill themselves for him during training camp was that we knew he was working himself even harder than he worked us. He also taught me by example that it's okay to bring your emotions to the field, that it's not a sign of weakness.

Coach is a perfect illustration of the fact that mentors don't have to be your buddy or Mr. Miyagi from The Karate Kid to be exactly what you need. Some mentors give fire and brimstone speeches and teach you things personally. Others lead by example and expect you to pick up the lessons on your own. But I think there are some qualities that all terrific mentors have in common:

- They've been where you are. A mentor should be at least familiar with the challenges you face. That doesn't mean they have to be in the profession you aspire to, though it doesn't hurt. But they should have something in common with you, because they will understand your situation better. That can mean coming from the same kind of poor background, growing up in the same town, coming from a military family, having a similar physical disability or many other things.

- They see something you don't know you're capable of. A mentor might see some ability or talent in you that you've never even thought about. That can open new doors for you in college, career and life.

- They set high standards. The best mentors ask more of you than you will of yourself. They're not trying to be your friends, though when all's said and done you may have more affection for them than you do for many of your friends. Instead, they'll push you to the point where you're cursing them and wishing you'd never met them…but afterwards, you'll be grateful. A great mentor sees potential in you that no one else can see and doesn't let you settle for less than bringing out every last bit of it.

• They explain. When I was trying to make myself into a pro football receiver, there was so much I didn't know. I would tip defenders to pass plays by how I looked back at the quarterback or lined up, for instance. I was lucky enough to have mentors who taught me how to fix what I was doing wrong. They took me aside and patiently showed me how I could do the small things that real professionals did. They helped me turn myself from an over-the-hill recruit into a real player.

• They know when to let you fail. Sometimes, the best thing a mentor can do is share his or her knowledge then turn you loose to fall on your ass. When we're young, we often suffer from know-it-all disease; we think we've got the world figured out when in fact we don't have a clue. And we won't listen to anyone who tries to tell us otherwise. A wise mentor knows that the best way to learn is often to fail, and that failure doesn't have to crush us. I think the reason that people fear failure is that they fear others will judge them by their failures. But a great mentor doesn't judge. He or she picks you back up, asks good questions and keeps teaching.

JANET: But what if you don't know anyone who would make a good mentor? Then choose someone you don't know but admire, like a sports hero, a political leader or an artist. Figure out what that person has done to become successful and try to emulate her or him. Having a great example is just as important as having a great mentor.

## IF YOU HAD A MENTOR, BE ONE

In my career as a speaker and public figure, I've been blessed to have many people, especially kids, come up to me and tell me that my story inspired them to keep going or to do something they had thought they couldn't. You can do the same thing, even if you haven't had a movie made about your life. If you were lucky enough to have a fantastic mentor in your youth, someone who helped set the direction for your life, then pay it forward. Become a mentor for somebody else. Become a Big Brother or Big Sister.

I think being a mentor is real-ly a gift that you give to yourself. It's such a wonderful experience to serve someone else and know that you're making a positive difference in the life of a young person. In this age, when so much is changing right under our feet—technology, politics, the job market—I think it's vital for

young people today to have someone they can turn to who can say, "Yeah, I've been there, and this is how this part of the world works."

More than that, mentoring just feels good. I think we're built to serve. It's part of our DNA. The tennis great Arthur Ashe said, "True heroism is remarkably sober, very undramatic. It is not the urge to surpass all others at whatever cost, but the urge to serve others at whatever cost." That's what you become when you mentor someone: a hero.

## END ZONE

**Things to think about & do after finishing this chapter**

- Find and thank any mentors you may have had when you were coming up in the world.
- If you're struggling with changing times right now, write down the names of people who you think would make good mentors and reach out to them.
- Get involved in organizations like The National Mentoring Partnership (www.mentoring.org).
- Think about areas in which you could mentor a young person and how that would give gifts back to you.

WHO ARE YOUR MENTORS?

_____

_____

_____

_____

# CHAPTER EIGHT

# YOU, ACT TWO

*"Be thankful for what you have; you'll end up having more. If you concentrate on what you don't have, you will never, ever have enough."*

— Oprah Winfrey

Landscape designer, teacher, pro football player, radio and TV broadcaster, mortgage broker, fitness coach, motivational speaker—I've reinvented myself a lot of times in my life.  So has Janet.  That's how you stay fresh and vital and roll with changing times.

 F. Scott Fitzgerald famously said there are no second acts in American lives, but he was from a time long before the Internet, globalization and the contractor economy.  These days, change comes faster than ever: corporate mergers and acquisitions, blended families, mobile technology, healthcare reform, you name it.  The ground can shift under your feet so fast that the career you thought was going to be your calling for the best 40 years is suddenly a line on your resume.  The days of my father, who worked at Westinghouse for decades, are long gone.  When conditions shift, you've got to be able to shift right back at them by reinventing yourself.  You've got to be able to start Act Two of your life—or Act Three, Four and beyond.

 I reinvented myself so many times I've lost count.  Each time, my intention was to make the situation work over the long term, but that rarely pans out.  You've got to have a soft place to land in the back of your mind.  Even when I did the ultimate reinvention—from school- teacher to pro football special teams player—I knew that even though I loved the game and wanted to play ten years, odds were I would only last one or two.  The NFL's tough; younger guys are always gunning for your job.  That I lasted four years and qualified for an NFL pension was a small miracle.

 Leaving a pro sports career is horribly hard for many athletes.  Some have a really rough time with it.  The entire scene is intoxicating: the adoring fans, the fat paychecks, the free meals at local restaurants, the camaraderie of the locker room, going to war with a bunch of guys who know exactly how hard you're working because they're doing the same.  It's hard to give up.  That's why so many players in every sport try to hang on past the time when they should leave, and often embarrass themselves.  They don't know what they'll do with their lives once they're no longer playing.  Imagine being 40 years old and being told your lifelong career is over!

## JANET'S WORDS FOR WOMEN

*I don't call it reinvention. I call it "hitting the refresh button" like you do on your Web browser. You're not tearing everything down and starting from scratch. It's giving yourself a new look, a new direction, or a new attitude.*

*Now, that doesn't mean you wear jeans that don't cover your crack, like you're a 17-year-old. You don't get plastic surgery that makes you look like a wax dummy. You don't need to do that. Take care of yourself. Be fit. Change your look. Try something new. Do something about who you are and want to be. Sometimes, that's all you need to give yourself a new lease on life.*

## IT'S ABOUT BELIEVING

I was lucky. I'd already been doing so many things after I retired that it wasn't as hard for me to create a post-football Act Two. No matter what act I'm on I get no greater satisfaction than being Mr. Mom…only it took me 47 years to get that to that point. After I left the game, I found the confidence to get out and ask people questions as a broadcaster. That was my new incarnation, and for a while it worked. I enjoyed it. Then I did something else, and then something else. As an author and speaker, I think I'm on Act Five, but so what? Sometimes it takes a while to find your calling, what really brings out the best in you. I was always good at playing to the crowd and firing them up, so being a speaker for big companies is a natural.

The key for me was the same as for anyone: building up confidence and self-belief. You can do almost anything you want to if you have the confidence. Look at the Dallas Mavericks. They went into the NBA Finals this year underdogs to the superstar-packed Miami Heat, and partway through Game Two it looked like they were done. But then they started believing they were the better team, and their pride came through. They saw the Heat celebrating prematurely and said, "We don't think so." They believed, they stepped up and from then on, they dominated and are world champions.

Self-reinvention doesn't have to be about staying in the same genre or field that you're in now, especially with changes in certain industries. The world is full of people who went from being corporate managers to making guitars, auto mechanics to farmers, stay-at-home moms to attorneys. Sometimes, the wilder the jump, the greater the satisfaction. Getting that far out of your comfort zone and excelling is a major adrenaline rush. That's why you find so many people who left the security of a corporate job for the high-wire act of self-employment who swear they will never go back. We thrive on novelty and challenge.

Janet reinvented herself from a international-level gymnast to a top collegiate coach. Now she's a businesswoman. By working hard, believing and surrounding yourself with people who bring out the best in you, you can create a new act.

## FEAR: THE GREAT COP-OUT

JANET: I only knew myself as an athlete, a gymnast on the U.S. World Gymnastics team. Then I blew out my knee was I was 18 years old and just like that, my career was essentially over. When you're at an elite athletic level in international sports, there's a time when you either make a move and become Olympic-caliber or you fall to the side. My time came and I was injured, so I was left behind. That was the risk, I knew it and I accepted it grudgingly.

But who was I if I wasn't a gymnast? What was my identity? How do you reinvent yourself at 19, an age when most people haven't even invented themselves the first time yet? My parents were going through a divorce, so I really didn't have anybody I could turn to for advice. I became a gymnastics coach because a gymnastics academy in State College, Pennsylvania needed a director and I was available, but I really didn't know what came next.

I tried out for the Penn State tennis team and almost made it, but they saw me as a liability because of my knee. Then I tried one- and three-meter diving, and I was good at it, which isn't really shocking because I had been a gymnast and had great body control and spatial awareness. I made the Penn State diving team and broke all sorts of

*"The reinvention of daily life means marching off the edge of our maps."*

— Bob Black

school records in just three months in the sport. So now I was diving during the school year, teaching gymnastics during the summers and wondering what I was going to do with my next act in life...not realizing that this was my next act!

Then I met some people from South Africa who had watched me coach. They said, "You really know how to get things from people. Would you like to come to South Africa coach gymnastics for us?" That really opened my eyes. I had been thinking of myself as a diver who was just coaching gymnastics to make extra money. But now I really thought about it. I was good at coaching. I did know how to bring out the best in my students, even more than they thought they had in them. And I loved it.

Not long after that, in 1976 (the same year Vince tried out for the Eagles) karma kicked in and I was offered a gymnastics coaching job at the University of Pennsylvania. This was amazing. I was in my senior year as an undergraduate and I was an average student. I was hyper, couldn't sit still and always thought I was dumb. I never believed I could get good grades. Yet here I was being offered a coaching position at an Ivy League school!

I handwrote a resume and sent it to the university. At my interview, they asked me how I would handle the team and I told them. They said, "You're hired." Just like that, at 22 years old, I was head coach at Penn, the youngest head gymnastics coach in Division One athletics. Imagine that!

I had been afraid before I went for that interview, but I didn't let it stop me from reinventing myself. Fear holds you back. Trying and failing is a lot better than staying where you are and being miserable. At least you can take pride in having the guts to go out on a limb. As the saying goes, that's where the fruit is.

## REINVENTION 101

VINCE: Belief is one of the prerequisites of self-reinvention, but there are others. It doesn't matter if you are satisfied with where you are today or aching to move on to something else. At some point, you'll want to make a change or be forced to by a pink slip or some other crisis. When that time comes, you'd better know how to do it. You may even find yourself planning for a move far into the future and wanting to be ready for some unspecified opportunity. Either way, here's a playbook of some things you must think about and do before Act Two:

- **Passive or proactive?** Will you sit back and wait for change to come to you or will you go out and find it? Either one is a valid choice. Sometimes, when you're in a good spot, you can afford to bide your time, make plans and wait until circumstances force your hand. Some of the best small businesses launched only after unemployment left the founder no other choice. So it's okay to stay where you are, do your research and lay in resources like a squirrel storing nuts for winter. Or maybe you're ready to move now—to go out and stir things up by giving yourself no choice, quitting your job or moving to another city. Either way is fine, but choose one or the other. The choice will define everything else about your next act .

- **Watch for opportunities.** Read the newspaper and the trades in your industry. Network and attend important events. Talk to people. Watch the Internet. Set up news alerts. Keep on top of what's going on in the area where you want your next act to take place. You never know when something you read last Thursday will connect up with a rumor from a colleague and bingo. You've got your big idea and your next move. One of Coach Vermeil's favorite wall posters said, "An opportunity is worth to a person exactly what their preparation enables them to make of it!" The opportunities I blew were those where I felt entitled or was ill-prepared. The ones I seized were the ones I worked my butt of to get.

- **Consider the timing and impact.** Sometimes, you can't just run off and reinvent yourself. If you're single and nobody depends on you, go for it with our blessings. But if you have a family and a mortgage, or if we're in the middle of the worst economic downturn since the Depression, think twice. It would be lovely to believe that you could chuck your six-figure paycheck to follow your heart and become a worm farmer, but maybe you can't. Not right now. You should always be thinking about who you're affecting. Will they support you? Will they pay an unacceptable price? Also, are the conditions right for your idea?

• **Talk to everybody.** When you make your move, make friends. People in your new world are the best source of insight, tips and ideas. Pick the brains of everyone you can. Always reciprocate by buying dinner, buying drinks or sending thank you gifts or handwritten notes. But remember that for the most part people love to share what they know. Ask away and make sure you either take notes or have a perfect memory.

• **Don't expect to be comfortable.** Whatever you decide to reinvent yourself as, you're not going to feel comfortable. You'll be scared witless. There will be a steep learning curve. You'll feel like fish out of water. You'll wonder if you did the right thing and contemplate running back to your old boss, begging him to take you back. Calm down. It's okay. That's normal. You're living without a net now, and it's understandable that you'd be a little uncomfortable. Take it as a sign that you're really stepping out into the unknown and growing. Embrace the fear and you'll get past it faster than you think.

• **What's your five-year vision?** You won't always have a plan when you reinvent yourself, but it helps. Otherwise, how will you know your next move? Even if you have to react in a split-second to a sudden opportunity like a surprise job offer, after the fact you can say, "All right, I'm taking it, where does this lead me in five years?"

# INVINCIBLE MOMENT

*It's about time I shared my Invincible Moment with you, so here it is:*

*The last time I had run track was in junior high, where I was coached by one of the best, Marty Stern, a diminutive quarter-miler who became a legendary high school and college coach known affectionately as Uncle Marty. When I was a high school senior, with a severe case of senioritis, I was all set to go to West Chester State Teachers College and get a shot at playing football there. One of my former teachers, Walt Buechle, was freshman coach there.*

*Coach George Corner had just agreed to coach track and field at the High School level and he convinced me to come out for the team. No way I could turn my back on my mentor, so I promptly said yes and told coach I wanted be a pole-vaulter. Heck, I used to pole vault over clothes-lines and across the crick (not creek) in the Project where I grew up, so why not?*

*I beat the school record of 11'2" the first time I picked up a pole. Coach saw such potential in me that he was able to score one of those new fiberglass poles for me. I really began to soar. Eventually I set the school record that still stands, 12'9", and qualified for the Pennsylvania State Track and Field Championships after winning the District 1 Championship.*

*George auditioned me to three local Division One colleges to see if we could grab some scholarship money, but all three turned us down. I was devastated. I knew I had the potential to go higher but they were not convinced. Eventually, however, I got the last laugh.*

*On Father's Day, 1964, the Track and Field Meet of Champions was held, attracting an elite field from the Greater Philadelphia Area. Since I was the District 1 pole vault champ I was invited...and went head to head with the three guys that I was passed over for by the colleges. Was I pumped? I was so fired up I didn't need a pole to clear the bar. I used*

one anyway, and jumped nearly two feet past my personal best. I hit
14'6"; the world record was just over 16 feet! Not only did I get the gold
medal but I also beat the three guys who had scholarships in their pockets.

Right on the spot I was approached by the head coaches from the
three colleges who told me I was not good enough for their program. All of
a sudden there was scholarship money available. Are you kidding me?
Then up walked Lou Nicastro, the head coach for St. Joseph's University.
In a very calm way, he asked me if I'd like to be a Hawk. I was with my
Dad, we looked at each other, and we accepted.

What a Father's Day gift: a free ride to one the most prestigious
Jesuit colleges in the U.S. My dad and I cried like babies, and as he
hugged me he whispered those words he so rarely spoke: "I love you
Vincie, and I am so proud of you!"

## SO MUCH MORE THAN ON THE FIELD

Most of all, reinvention is hard. You'll have to do things you had no idea
you could do. But it really is worth it. People have no idea how hard it
was for me to reinvent myself as an NFL player. I had physical ability, sure.
I'd always been a terrific natural athlete. But there is a LOT more that goes
into playing in the pros.

For one thing, the demands on your body are incredible. I had to
start a training and stretching regimen with Gus Hoefling, who was a mar-
tial arts master and a flexibility guru and trained baseball stars like Mike
Schmidt and Steve Carlton. He said he saw a hunger in me and Dennis
Franks that he didn't see in other guys. So we worked with him to become
more limber and prevent injuries.

I had to learn to lift weights. Dennis taught me how. I had only
been a track and field guy up to that point, and while I would do body
weight work like pushups and pull-ups, I had never gotten on a bench and
pumped barbells before. Denny showed me proper form, how to choose the
right amount of weight and the like.

The most difficult thing was learning the jargon of the NFL under
tremendous stress. The game has its own language and you have ten sec-

1958

An All Star in the Snow. That's me on the left with sneakers wrapped with friction tape for cleats.

A confused, shy, and withdrawn 7th grader looking for direction.

Easter was always special to The Cantwell Family. At the annual Rittenhouse Square Easter Parade we won "Best Dressed Family" 3 years in a row … And we were "retired" to the Hall of Fame.

The summers were always highlighted by entering baby parades, like Mom didn't have enough to do. At the Ocean City, NJ, baby parade our theme was "The Fleet's In" and we came out winners. Tina, #9, was not born yet.

Vince's Dad, Kingie, on his "Field of Dreams" in 1940, at the pig farm his Dad owned.

Some of the Cantwell family on the Mike Douglas Show and a young Barbara Walters.

A Happy Senior at Interboro HS who found his way thanks to his Mentor George Corner.

Vince's Mom, Almira 'Big Al' Sage in 1937, star shortstop with "The Bobbie's" who barnstormed the East Coast prior to WWII.

1970-71
USA WOMEN'S
NATIONAL GYMNASTIC
TEAM

SOUVENIR
ROSTER

Here I was, at the age of 15, competing for a spot on the 1970-1971 USA Women's Gymnastics National Team. Against all odds I made the team and I traveled all over the world proudly wearing USA on my uniform.

This is me doing a floor exercise at National Competition in 1970-1971 in Colorado.

I reinvented myself from being a gymnast to a diver at Penn State University where I set all of their records.

I was a junior at St. Joes here flying down the pole vault runway.

Here's the Cantwell Kids, all 9 of us, at the Philadelphia Art Museum in 1975.

The Nittany Lion is the Penn State mascot and he's keeping me warm during a diving competition.

Coach Corner gave me a shot as a first year senior which is like being a free agent in the NFL.

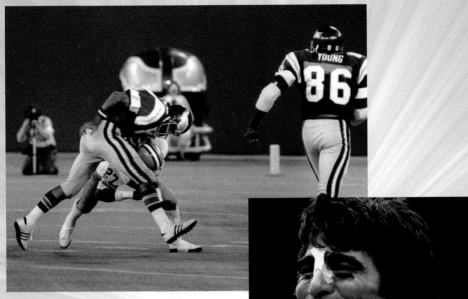

One of my catches I made against
the Browns in my first pre-season
hoping to impress the coaches.

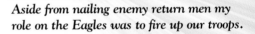

Aside from nailing enemy return men my
role on the Eagles was to fire up our troops.

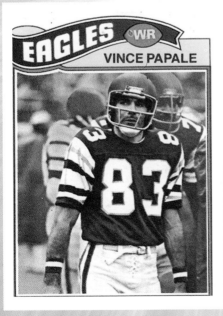

Can you believe that I even had a
rookie card! To me that is priceless.

Leading my team in pre-game
stretches as Captain of The Special
Teams in 1977.

One of your greatest rewards is knowing you got the job done.

Without a doubt one of my favorites ... sharing your glory with your teammates.

Denny Franks and me celebrating after a big play to seal the deal. The "Last Laugh" hangs in the Pro Football Hall of Fame in Canton, Ohio.

Here's and oldie but goodie from a Golf Outing for one of my favorite charities and I now happen to be on their Board of Directors.

Our wedding reception in 1993 was a blast and we are surrounded here by Coach Vermeil; NFL Legends Ron Jaworski, Bruce Laird and Denny Franks; and a few of Vince's friends.

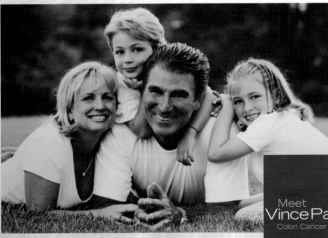

Very proud to be a national spokesperson for Colon-Rectal Cancer Awareness and this is from a 2006 campaign.

Janet, Vinny, Gabriella and me in a family portrait (2001) two days before my successful colon cancer surgery.

A happy moment with
two men who helped
shape my future, my
Dad and Coach Corner.

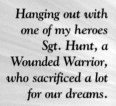

Hanging out with
one of my heroes
Sgt. Hunt, a
Wounded Warrior,
who sacrificed a lot
for our dreams.

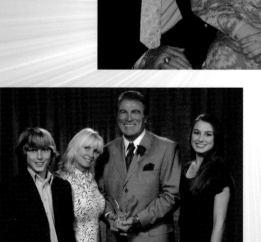

Coach Vermeil and
me on the red carpet
at the premier of
Invincible at the
Ziegfeld Theater in
NYC - 2006.

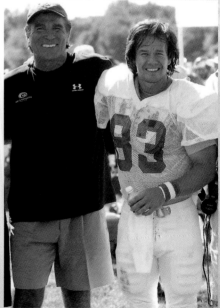

A proud Papale Family at my recent
induction into the St. Josephs University
Sports Hall of Fame.

I was so impressed with
Mark Wahlberg and here we are on set.
He promised that he would make me,
and Philly, proud and delivered with a
performance worthy of an Oscar.

onds in the huddle to understand and process the information into instructions on what to do when the ball is snapped. That was hard for me, and I put in countless hours of study.

I also had to reinvent myself as a celebrity, because when I made the team, I became one. I had to become a guy people would talk to.

> ### INVINCIBLE WISDOM
>
> *"It may be hard for an egg to turn into a bird: it would be a jolly sight harder for it to learn to fly while remaining an egg...you cannot go on indefinitely being just an ordinary, decent egg. We must be hatched or go bad."*
>
> — *C. S. Lewis*

Once at an event, a guy said to me, "I've never seen anything like you. You walk up to people, remember their names, thank them for coming, put them at ease and everybody leaves feeling wonderful." I thanked him but didn't tell him how much damned work had gone into making everyone feel at ease.

The lesson is that when you go for your next act, you'll have to do things you have never done. You'll feel overwhelmed and sometimes you'll feel like an idiot. But swallow your pride. Don't be afraid to say, "I don't know. Please teach me."

*When it gets cold and lonely on your sideline you have got to suck it up and go the extra degree.*

## NEW WORLD MEANS NEW OPPORTUNITY

**JANET:** When Vince and I were looking for a photographer to shoot the photos for this book, we weren't happy with anyone we found. We took off one day to an old, beautiful part of Philadelphia and saw a street market, so we walked through it. In one of the booths we saw some gorgeous photography by a friendly young guy and asked him about his work. It turned out that he had left a six-figure job that he couldn't stand to become a photographer. And, like Vince, he was a St. Joe's grad. Right away, Vince and I knew we had found our guy, and team, Russ Brown and his partner Stacey Granger. Now they are shooting our family portrait. There's that karma again.

That's what reinvention is. It's throwing yourself out there and seeing what happens. It's an adventure. Whether you do it today or in five years, you're going to open up new worlds. You'll get the freedom to fail and learn, which is a little like being a kid all over again. And you'll wind up surprised at what you're capable of. After all, if you do it once, you can do it again.

---

### END ZONE

**Things to think about & do after finishing this chapter**

■ Write down the research resources you should be following to learn as much as you can about your possible next act.

_____

_____

_____


■ List the people you'll talk to and learn from—and how you'll thank them.

_____

_____

_____

_____

---

## END ZONE *continued*

■ What's your five-year goal for your dream? If it's too soon to know, write down generally where you'd like to be in five years.

_____

_____

_____

_____

■ List some of the new skills you could start mastering today in preparation for an eventual second act.

_____

_____

_____

_____

■ Think about the people who might be impacted by your reinvention and what that impact might be.

_____

_____

_____

_____

_____

# CHAPTER NINE

# DEFINE YOUR ROLE

*"The way a team plays as a whole determines its success. You may have the greatest bunch of individual stars in the world, but if they don't play together, the club won't be worth a dime."*

— Babe Ruth

Sports is really all about role players. Think about it: there can only be so many superstars on a team. When you think about the great Chicago Bulls teams, you think about Michael Jordan. He was the superstar. As terrific a player as Scottie Pippin was, he was a role player. On a football team, there's a bigger roster as well as offensive, defensive and special teams squads, so there's more room for stars. So the Dallas Cowboys of the 1990s could have Troy Aikman, Michael Irvin and Emmet Smith all on the same team, all getting enough attention.

But even with multiple stars, nothing happens without role players doing their jobs and keeping out of the limelight. I was a role player during my years with the Eagles. I never scored a touchdown, and I only caught one official pass in a regular season game. My role was to cause chaos and flatten guy's on punts and kickoffs, and to be an energy source for my team-mates. When the right guys know their role and take pleasure in playing it for the good of the group, work becomes more fun and performance soars.

When I tried out for the Eagles, I knew I was a special teamer. Sure, it would have been great to catch a touchdown pass in the NFL, but that wasn't in the cards. I didn't go in seeing myself as a wideout or a kick return guy. Ironically, I wound up leading the team in receptions at that brutal first Vermeil training camp. But I knew that I was a role player, and that was fine with me. I just wanted to be on the team and I was willing to do any-thing to make myself valuable enough that the coaches would put me on the roster. That was my role, and I was good at it.

## JANET'S WORDS FOR WOMEN

*Women tend to become chameleons: we take on the coloring of what-ever situation we're in. That can be good, but it can also be bad. It's good when it lets you fit in and explore new things. But it's bad when it makes you hide who you really are in favor of not making waves or not bruising someone's ego. If your natural role is to stand out or to be the leader, then don't blend in. Instead of being a chameleon, be a peacock! Women have to learn not to hide our gifts and our ideas because men or other women won't like them. We need to have the courage to step into our roles and be the best we can be.*

# What's Your Role in the World?

In the real world (meaning the world outside of pro sports), there are very few superstars. There are a few celebrities, some CEOs, a few top doctors and lawyers and politicians who might be able to write their own ticket no matter what the rules say, but the vast majority of us don't have that option. We need to know what our role is. If you don't know what your role is in your life, you need to figure it out.

When the world changes quickly, your role defines who you are and what you can do. That's an anchor in times when you might lose sight of what really matters or what you stand for. Look at what's been happening around us since 2008! Nearly twice as many Americans are unemployed than were jobless in 2006. That's devastating not just on an economic level but on a personal level. Associated Press reporter Jocelyn Noveck called job loss "the new identity theft" in a 2009 article. An unemployed MBA interviewed for a Spring 2011 article for CPG Jobs said, "It feels as though my entire life has been ripped away from me, my identity, my friends. To make it worse, some of my friends have gotten new jobs and their backgrounds aren't nearly as good as mine. I tell you, this is really hard to take."

In the world of business and career, people need to know where they fit in, what's expected of them or what to expect of themselves. When you don't know your role and your world gets turned upside down with a layoff notice or the news that your company is going under, how do you define yourself? How do you communicate your value to a new company? It's hard enough to find work these days when you can paint a clear picture of who you are; why make it harder for a potential employer to figure out who you are and what you can do?

It's vital that you define your role in the part of the world that you live in. Are you a utility player? There's nothing wrong with that. Teams don't win without players like that, the hard-nosed ones who do all the little things well. If you've been carrying on without knowing your role, and you've been frustrated that what you're doing doesn't fit your expectations, something's got to change. Define your role and you define the person you are today and the person you can become tomorrow.

## WHAT IS A ROLE?

It's not a job. That's a common misconception. There's nothing special about being a sales executive, marketing manager or factory foreman. What is special is how you perform those jobs. My definition of a role is very simple:

> INVINCIBLE WISDOM
>
> *"The first duty of a human being is to assume the right functional relationship to society—more briefly, to find your real job, and do it."*
>
> — *Charlotte Perkins Gilman*

### *It's how you create the value that improves results for everyone in the group.*

My role on the Eagles wasn't "special teams daredevil," it was "sparkplug who plays at 100 mph all the time and never stops hustling." By playing that way, I didn't just make plays. I established a baseline for the acceptable level of energy and commitment. Coach Vermeil made an example of my style of play and work ethic, and while there were a few guys who took offense at my being singled out, most ended up inspired by what I was doing. That's why they voted me captain of Special Teams.

Do you know how you create value at your workplace or in your community? Are you the father figure who gives good advice? Are you the quality watchdog who's always making sure that people get what they pay for? The supervisor with a knack for teaching young upstarts the skills they need? Look at the things that you do in your job, family or community that make other people's work or lives better. That's your role. When you know what your role is, you can see what you're working with when you reach out to others. They'll see the ways you create value, not just the job titles on your resume.

**JANET:** My role is a little different from Vince's. I'm the business-woman. I'm the dealmaker. Anybody who underestimates me because I'm petite and blonde is in for a big surprise. That's one of my roles. I have many:

- **Mother** — I'm not my children's friend. I'm a mentor, a counselor, a teacher and a disciplinarian. I'll be their friend when they're adults.

- **Spouse** — I'm here to complement and encourage Vince, but also to be tough on him when he needs to step up and be everything that he can be. I make him better and he makes me better. He lets me be me and doesn't try to change me. I have my own career in real estate and my own identity, and I'll never give those up. That's why we have a great marriage.

- **Businesswoman** — You can be feminine and still be suc-cessful. For example, I had a contractor come to paint my house, and he fed me a story to pay him more: his wife was a domestic and couldn't get a job, the holidays were coming and so on. I said, "I sell real estate, I manage our rental properties, I manage Vince, I cook, and I'm a mom. Your wife can't get a job? Have her call me; I'll give her a job." Not another word about wanting more money.

I think it's really important for each person in a relationship to have a distinct role. You can complement each other, but don't be afraid to each have your territory where you shine.

# INVINCIBLE MOMENT

*Michael Sandler, author of* Barefoot Running: How to Run Light and Free By Getting In Touch With the Earth, *was a former speed skater and professional cyclist turned activist. In 2006, weeks before a planned inline skating world record attempt from Los Angeles to New York to raise awareness about ADD/ADHD, Michael experienced an accident that changed his life forever.*

    *While he was inline skating down Boulder Creek Trail, in Boulder, Colorado, a father and toddler stepped in front of Michael's path. To avoid a collision, Michael jumped backwards, landing hard on concrete. The result was ugly: a broken arm, broken hip and shattered femur. Doctors told him that he might not be able to keep his leg and that if he did, he might not be able to walk again. He most definitely would, they insisted, never be able to run again. Ten subsequent knee surgeries left him with a one-inch leg length discrepancy between his legs, a titanium femur and hip, shocking scars and a grim outlook. He was too weak to even raise his head from the hospital bed.*

    *But Michael never gave in. One week out after leaving his living room hospital bed, he set the record for finishing the Bolder Boulder 10K on crutches—with a broken arm. Two weeks later, he completed the Denver Half Marathon on crutches, the only person ever to do it.*

    *Gradually, he worked himself into barefoot running. The first day, he ran 100 yards, and then iced his feet for two days. The second time, he ran 200 yards, and then iced his feet for another two days. That pattern continued for a while until slowly, his feet began to adapt. Barefoot running gradually led him back to health, activating tiny muscle groups that running in shoes did not. He ran through snow and across barren rock in the desert sun. Today, Michael routinely runs 50+ miles barefoot and averages 80-100 miles barefoot running a week. Rather than run, he says, he "dances." He also speaks to audiences of runners and people recovering from injury to show them firsthand what is possible.*

*More on Michael's story can be found at www.runbare.com.*

# HOW TO FIGURE OUT YOUR ROLE

The key to figuring out your role is figuring out how you bring value to every situation at work or at home. Try asking yourself a series of tough questions and answering them as honestly as you can:

- What am I best at?

- What do I do that helps other people perform better?

- What do I do that seems to inspire other people or make them happier?

- What job or pursuit combines my best skills and talents with my ability to improve things for others?

- Am I spending most of my time in that job or pursuit or doing something unrelated?

- How can I change my situation so that I spend more of my time creating value?

When you find that thing that combines the best of talent and skill along with your ability to lead and inspire, you've found your role.

## Write Your Role Here

---

# HOW KNOWING YOUR ROLE HELPS YOU

So you know your role in the world. So what? How is that going to help you deal with changing times or get back on your feet after a job loss or some other disaster crushes you? When you know your role, you know where you're most valuable, so you can apply yourself in that area and quit wasting time doing other things that don't create value. You also have a stronger sense of self and self-worth, so you're less likely to wind up depressed and feeling helpless when things go south. Some of the other ways in which knowing your role can make a big difference:

- It gives you perspective. When your identity is tied to a job and that job ends, your identity goes with it. But when you're all about that value-creating role, the end of a job doesn't have the same impact. For example, I was devastated when I was cut by the Eagles before the 1978 season in favor of younger, faster guys. I cried like a baby when it happened. But I had perspective; I knew my role hadn't changed. I was still the guy who could inspire other people with my infectious energy. As part of that self-image, I stayed in great shape (thanks in part to 76ers coach Doug Collins), and when the Eagles called later in the season to rehire me, I was ready.

- It teaches you to value even the small things. You don't have to be rich or famous to make an important contribution to the world—and in fact, it's often the people doing the overlooked work who contribute more than anybody else. If you value the things that come from people performing their roles with dedication and pride—the barista who makes you a fantastic cup of cappuccino every morning or the postal worker who looks after your house when you're away—you're more likely to value your own small contributions to a better world.

- It grounds you. We live in a society that's addicted to fame, which is idiotic. If you think fame buys you happiness, watch almost any reality show (The Biggest Loser is an exception). But that doesn't stop most people from worshipping fame, money and power. The trouble comes when you set your standards to that level: if you don't become a millionaire with your face on the cover of Time, you're a failure. But most people will never get to that level; doing so takes talent and brains but also incredible luck and connections. Why waste years envying and trying to emulate the rich and famous when they're no happier—and in many cases, much less happy—than you? Do the things you do, as the song says, and be who you are.

- It makes you more resilient. Losing your job can be crippling to your ego and future. There are plenty of people out there who can't get jobs because they are overqualified, and companies are afraid to take a chance on them for fear that as soon as the economy improves, they'll be gone. In that kind of situation, if you can tolerate part-time work until things improve, it helps lessen the burden.

## Roles Change, Change With Them

With all this talk about things that can't be taken away from you, roles do change. I went from being a 30-year-old rookie to special teams captain in two years. That changed my role. Instead of being just a demolition derby on the field, I was now an example. Your role can change with little warn-

> INVINCIBLE WISDOM
>
> *"Everybody has a responsible role to play and we all do better when we work together."*
>
> — Bill Clinton

ing. When it does, you'd better know how you will create value in your new reality—because it won't always be the same.

I've been a teacher, football player, speaker, personal trainer, mortgage broker and a few other things for good measure. Those have been my jobs. They aren't my roles. The role that's carried over into every line of work has been that I tried to lead by inspiration and example, doing what I thought was right and sticking to that. I've had to make adjustments because with each new situation comes a new need for value, but the basics have stayed the same. I'm a regular guy who brings everything he has to everything he does and tries to make everybody smile. That's my role.

Your role today is just that—your role today. It might stay the same for the next 40 years, or it might need to change as the times change. Yesterday's corporate computer jockey can be tomorrow's Internet startup guru, and that change demands some changes in how he creates value for others. As your life takes its twists and turns, be ready to make adjustments in the role it's best for you to play. That way, no matter what life throws you, you'll have a strong core where you can't be shaken.

## END ZONE

**Things to think about & do after finishing this chapter**

■ Write down what you think your role is today at home and at work.

_____

_____

_____

■ Ask people you trust how they think you create value for others.

_____

_____

_____

■ Speculate: How could you change your job or career to best blend your talents with the way you bring value to others?

_____

_____

_____

■ What is your identity if you take away your business cards, job title, resume and education?  Who are you?

_____

_____

_____

■ Write up a sample resume based not on past positions but on the ways that you create value for others—as a teacher, a coach, an example, a hard worker, a creative brainstormer and so on.

_____

_____

_____

# Chapter Ten

# Play With Passion

"Without passion, you don't have energy.
Without energy, you have nothing."

— Donald Trump

A few years ago, long after I had been out of football and moved on in my life, a friend contacted me about broadcasting for the Arena Football League. He knew that I had done broadcasts before and could handle myself in the booth, and probably figured that my name recognition would get a few more fans to tune in. I thought it was a great idea; I missed the game. But there was a problem, he said. "We can't pay you very much."

I told him I would do it anyway. "I'm not doing it for the dollars," I replied. "I'm doing it for the love of the game." The Arena League isn't a fraction as big or popular as the NFL, though it's been around since 1987 and it's survived through some predictably rough times. So I knew they couldn't pay me like I was doing Monday Night Football. It didn't matter. I never did the final three games of the season duen to my crazy appearance schedule but that's not the point. People who are all about money probably thought I was crazy, but I didn't care. I was glad to be a part of pro football team again, because it's my passion. And my teammate Ron Jaworski is GM. Heck, today I'm a season ticket holder for my local Arena team, the Philadelphia Soul. These guys play for the love of the game.

Passion is such a vital part of a fulfilling and happy life, and I think it's also the first thing to go when times get tough. That's unfortunate, because passion is what keeps you going when change comes fast and furious and you're hanging on for dear life. Passion is the love you have for something in your life that fuels you. When you're passionate about something, you'll do it for nothing but the pleasure of it. That's the way I felt when I made the Eagles. I was grateful for the money, but I would have played for meal money.

Other than my wife and my children, I have never loved anything more than being out there on that football field, with the crowd on my side, playing as one unit with my teammates, making good things happen. It was magic. But I also loved being a teacher and coach, broadcaster, and I love being a motivational speaker today. If you're lucky, you can have a lot of passions in your life.

## PASSION IS POWER

In changing, unsure times, passion can give you the energy and power to get past fear and depression and do what needs to be done. You know the old saying, "Do what you love and you'll never work a day in your life"? People who do that are working with passion. Even in a changing job market, if you find your passion for a line of work you're much more likely to get the job or advance. Passion moves people. It moves mountains. No matter how rational and logical we like to think we are, we're emotional beings. When we see someone giving everything they have for something they love, we want to reward that person. Heck, we want to be like them.

**JANET:** Passion is love to an end. It's about going after something 110%. It's about fun with a goal in mind. I used to have my own construction company. How many women own construction companies? It's an industry where women get taken advantage of a lot. But I wanted to do it, so I did. When you're passionate about something, you just go for it and find a way to make it work. That's exactly what I did.

**VINCE:** My tenure with the Eagles is a perfect example of what Janet's talking about. As relatively unskilled as I was as a football player compared to my teammates who had played elite college ball, nobody ever doubted my passion. Passion was what kept me playing even when it looked like I would spend my life as a teacher and counselor. Passion got me to try out for the Philadelphia Bell, pushed me through Coach Vermeil's killer training camp, and made me play with such abandon that Coach used me as an example of how to "leave it all on the field." Without my passion, I doubt that I would have ever played a single down in the NFL.

When you care so deeply about something, you get very clear on what's important. I remember getting a call a few years ago from St. Joseph's University, my alma mater, asking me if I would come and get hit in the face with a pie for charity. Miss a chance to get whipped cream all over my gorgeous mug? Never! I went, had a great time and signed autographs for an hour and a half. Later, as I was resting my sore hand, the girl who had called said, "I never thought you would come." I said, "Are you kidding? I'm just another guy from St. Joe's!"

I didn't get a dime to appear. Could I have made more with my time speaking for a paying group? Of course. That wasn't the point. The point was that I wanted to give something back to one of the places that gave so much to me. That was important. Money never entered my

mind. That's why passion is so powerful: it encourages you to care for
people and causes that matter, and
doing that can really come back to
help you down the line. The more
generous, caring and authentic you

*"Passion is the genesis
of genius."*

— *Tony Robbins*

are, the more other people are going to want to help you in the future.

## PASSION INSPIRES

I don't know about you, but when I see someone who's worked in the same
job or at the same craft for 50 years or so, always giving every job his best
without ever getting his name in the paper or making a ton of money, I'm
inspired and moved. You probably know some people like this: teachers,
coaches, small business owners. I read about a barber in Los Angeles' old
Crenshaw District who's 94 and has been cutting hair since 1947—and as
far as I know, he's still going strong. That's incredible. That's having a passion for what you do and the people you serve, and it's inspiring.

You want to talk inspiration? Let me tell you about The Palestra.
It's a 9,000-seat stadium built in 1927 at the University of Pennsylvania
and it's all bleachers. When it's full, it feels like the fans are right on top
of you. In this area, we have the Big Five, an informal athletic conference
of universities that consists of Penn, La Salle, Saint Joseph's, Temple and
Villanova. The schools get together to play each other in a fiercely competitive in-house basketball tournament—but nobody wants to play in
the Palestra. Even if you're local, the passion and intensity of the fans is
intimidating. If you're from out of town, forget about it. Games have
been lost because teams melt down in that pressure cooker.

If you have passion for what you're doing, it moves other people to
want to help you, emulate you or buy what you're selling. Passion makes
us do better work than we would do if we were just going through the
motions; that's why a piece of furniture built by an individual craftsman
working in his country woodshop for the last 25 years is always going to
be of far better quality that something mass produced. When we love
what we do, that love comes through in attention to detail and the determination to make it as perfect as possible.

**What are you passionate about? Write down your passions:**

_____

_____

_____

_____

_____

## JANET'S WORDS FOR WOMEN

*I think a lot of women have a fairy tale idea of what life is going to be when they're married and have babies. Making that happen becomes their passion. But a passion based on bad information is more like a self-delusion. I see 15-year-old girls glamorizing the idea of having babies, but the ones who follow that path have a hard time ever knowing who they are. I know a woman who found her passion after she had kids when she was very young, then fell into something else by accident and discovered who she was. I love being a mom; it was something I chose, not something that happened by accident. It's important to know who you are before you give up other things to follow your passion.*

## INVINCIBLE MOMENTS

*Elle Swan shares a dramatic and moving Invincible Moment story:*
        *"After graduating from Oberlin College at age 22 I began a promising career in journalism. New York was everything I hoped it would be. I was happy, sure of my creative strength, and looking forward to making a name for myself. A couple of years later I received a call that my father had been found dead. He was my number one*

fan and hearing that news shattered me. I fell into an undiagnosed depression that instigated a downward spiral. I began medicating my grief with alcohol. As I drank more and more, I started acting more and more irresponsibly. I lost every writing job and eventually drifted 3,000 miles away from my family. I slept in shelters and bus stations to sleep.

"By 2000, I was living on the streets of Van Nuys, California. My addiction left me stranded with an alcoholic liver, a fat body, no job, no family, no friends, and nowhere to call home. Every day, I prayed for death. Then came Memorial Day, May 29, 2000. I was in a rundown part of Van Nuys, living with four addicts in a filthy, abandoned van with two wheels up on bricks. Two of my "roommates" were men, and the other was a 52-year-old prostitute who had become a mother figure to me. The night before, one of the guys had stolen something and bought a lot of drugs and alcohol. I did everything I could get my hands on.

"Eventually I passed out, and when I woke up the next morning, I was alone. Immediately, I felt the familiar, suffocating feeling of impending doom, only this time it was so much worse. It felt like I was falling into a dark pit. Finally, I was dying. But as my spirit was separating from my body, I screamed, 'God, NO!' Not only did my spirit slam back into my body, but in less than a minute, every detail about my life changed.

"Prior to that powerful moment, I was under the impression that I couldn't change the circumstances of my life. I believed that I was smaller than everything that was happening, and because of that, my life began to crush me. Today, as a result of what happened in that van, I am a lifestyle speaker and the President of 'Be Fit, Live Rich.' I've overcome every limitation that tore my life into shreds. I share my story so they others might see that they are invincible. We are bigger than what happens to us."

## THE PASSION-CENTERED PROFESSIONAL

I've never met Gary Zelesky, but he seems like a pretty amazing guy. He came from a background of terrible family abuse to become one of the most positive people you can imagine, and that energy comes through in his book, *The Passion-Centered Professional*. In it, Gary argues that passion, not money or position, should be at the heart of every decision you make in your career. He writes:

*The true development of passion is not a hobby, but a lifelong mission. Doing it right demands that you take your passion seriously and express it every day, even if it's in a small way. Passion is not an overnight fix, but something that needs to become a part of your career, just as integral as working with patients or clients...*

You might not believe that passion has a place in your professional life, but Gary argues that it should be central. If it is, he suggests, you'll enjoy greater income and productivity, more pleasure and more free time. Passion not only fuels outrageous effort and hard work, but it has a way of clearing out the crap. If you have to choose between one life path that's safe but humdrum and uninspiring and another that's thrilling and excites your passion, odds are you're going to go after the passion—IF you know what you're passionate about!

**JANET:** If you don't take the chance to go after your passion, you're probably going to be unfulfilled. How many people have you known who had a career path they were passionate about in school but didn't pursue because it wasn't practical? Plenty of people take the safe route so they'll "have something to fall back on." But what if you don't fall at all? What if you succeed? The problem is that you won't ever know if you only take the safe route.

With experience comes opportunity. Sometimes you don't know what you feel passionate about because you're just trying to survive. You have to make a living. But I think it's sad when people spend decades regretting that they didn't at least try to follow their passion, at least for a while. You're probably only going to get one chance, so why not try it?

## PASSION'S GREAT GIFT

The funny thing about passion is that it doesn't die. I loved football as a kid and an Eagles fanatic, but even though I didn't play seriously until I was in my twenties, that love never went away. It just lay dormant for a while as I created my life, and when I was ready to pick it back up it roared back to life.

That's true for you, too. Passion's great gift is that it never goes away. It's like a flower bulb in the ground that sleeps during winter, and then bursts out when spring comes and the air gets warmer. That something you dreamed about doing when you were 16 is still there, waiting to be called to life by a smell, a memory or a scene from an old movie.

That can be a curse, too, if you've had to make hard choices in life and leave your passion behind to be practical. That's the choice society usually forces us to make. We want to have adventures and change the world and our parents or teachers or spouses say, "No, you need to be sensible and realistic." And we stuff that passion into a box and stick it in the attic. But it never goes away. There are no garage sales for passion.

So that passion you've held onto is still in you. I'm not saying that you have to give up your career or run away from your responsibilities to follow it. Life isn't generally an either/or proposition. You can stay responsible, take care of your kids, pay your mortgage and still let your passion come through. Never got the chance to become a rock star? Form a band like my "last laugh" buddy Denny Franks did with a bunch of other over-the-hill guys and sing your heart out. Always wanted to start your own small business but went to work for the Man instead? Start your business online and see what happens. Maybe you can kiss the Man goodbye!

Ask yourself, what can I do with my passion? Write down some of your ideas here:

_____

_____

_____

_____

_____

_____

## I'M PASSIONATE…SO WHAT?

We live in a world that discounts our feelings and tells us passion doesn't matter.  You shouldn't dream.  You should just make money and follow the rules.  But no one ever did anything great doing that.  The fact is, passion isn't an inconvenient distraction from the business of having a rewarding life—it's the way to have a rewarding life!  When times are changing around you, passion is your anchor.  It reminds you what's important and unchanging when everything else is in flux.  Some of the ways that knowing and following your passion can help you make the most of life's changes:

- **It motivates you.**  Let's say you're stuck with a post-recession job that you don't want but can't afford not to have.  That's a recipe for depression and indifference, right?  Not if you tie the work to your passion for doing something else, like working with underprivileged kids or running marathons. If your job makes it possible for you to pursue a passion, you're going to do the best job you can, which can create some surprising opportunities.

- **It fuels reinvention.**  If you can't remake who you are as the circumstances of life evolve, then you're dead.  When you have a passion for a kind of work, a creative art or a cause, you have an anchor for those times when you need to find a fresh direction for your life.

- **It reminds you who you are.**  Job loss, divorce, relocation and other traumas can strip you of your identity for a while.  Who are you if you're not senior manager of Store #32 or John's wife?  Answer: you're a person with a passion for cooking, travel or helping kids with learning disabilities.  Having a passion that's alive and thriving helps you stay centered during chaos and hold on to who you are and what you believe.

- **It lets you go back in time.**  Not everybody gets this chance, but sometimes, your passion comes calling in a big way and you get to have the life you dreamed of years ago.  I did when I became a 30-year-old NFL rookie.  Susan Boyle did it when she went on Britain's Got Talent in 2009 and blew everybody away with that song from *Les Miserables*. Now she's a pop star. Hold on to your passion, because you never know when life will bring you an opportunity to make it live all over again, just like you did when you were a teenager. When that happens, you don't want to miss out.

## END ZONE

**Things to think about & do after finishing this chapter**

■ Write about a past passion that you passed on pursuing. Why?

_____

_____

■ What are you passionate about now?

_____

_____

■ How could you integrate that passion into your everyday life?

_____

_____

■ How could your passion make you better at what you do?

_____

_____

**Things I Can Do With My Passion**

_____

_____

_____

_____

# CHAPTER ELEVEN

# BE GOOD
## TO YOUR
# BODY AND MIND

*"It is health that is real wealth and not pieces of gold and silver."*

— Gandhi

Apart from the inevitable injuries that come when you're throwing your body around a football field with reckless abandon, I had always been remarkably healthy into middle age. Even when I was screened for colorectal cancer at 55, I felt perfectly fine. That is, until the doctor told me I had a cancerous polyp in my lower intestine.

Colon cancer is one of the most common forms of cancer, with about 100,000 new cases diagnosed each year. Nearly 50,000 people die of the disease per year. But it's also one of the most curable cancers—provided it's caught early while it's still in the form of lesions or polyps that attach to the intestinal wall. According to the American Cancer Society, 74% of people who catch their colon cancer at Stage One survive for at least five years after their diagnosis, and many are cured. So I was scared, but hopeful.

Ten years ago my surgeon removed my polyp right there during my colonoscopy (which I don't remember, because they give you a nice sedative that sends you right into dreamland) and told me later that it was a big one. A biopsy would confirm that it was indeed cancerous. That was the bad news. The good news was that we had caught it just in time, before it had grown. If that had happened, the cancer cells would have gotten into my colon wall and found their way into my liver. Then I would have been in serious trouble.

I was lucky. I didn't need chemo. I didn't need radiation. But I wasn't entirely out of the woods. My doctors did a CAT scan and found a growth on my thyroid. So the docs stuck needles into my throat while I was awake to biopsy the growth, which wasn't my idea of a good time, even with my throat numbed. They didn't like the looks of the cells; they could have been precancerous. So half my thyroid had to come out as well. Janet, always the dealmaker, tried to negotiate a twofer—one guy would operate on my colon while another cut on my thyroid.

No such luck. I went under the knife twice. Half my thyroid came out, another surgeon took out eighteen inches of my colon through my navel, and that was that. As of 2006, I was declared cancer-free and I've been clean ever since then.

## A NEW FOCUS ON HEALTH

From age 30 to 32, I could pretty much will my body to do anything, like those yogis who can slow their heart rates down to nothing. I had always felt a great synergy between mind and body. I thought that if my mind was strong, I simply wouldn't break down.

My experiences in football training camp backed me up. When I was training for the Olympic decathlon trials, I hated the mile run. But I loved training for football, because I knew that I was one of the fittest guys out there. When I got to training camp, I knew there would be so many psychological challenges thrown at me that I couldn't let myself get distracted. When the body breaks down, the mind follows. So I decided I was going to get into the best physical condition I could in the three months before training camp. That way, even when the grind wore me down physically, mentally I wouldn't falter.

Because of that, there was nothing that Coach Vermeil threw at me that I couldn't handle. If fatigue came, it was physical, not mental. I was functioning at 120% when everybody else was at 100%. The veterans would bitch and moan about the workouts, the reps and the sprints. But I loved it. I knew that the work was the key to meeting my potential.

But that was a different era. It's easy to take your health for granted when you can roll out of bed and run a 40-yard dash in 4.5 seconds. We ate steak and eggs before every game. Most guys quit working out when the season was done and came to camp out of shape (at least, until Coach Vermeil came along with his torturous camp and forced us all to stay in shape year-round). Supplements, yoga and all the other wellness and fitness ideas that you'll find in locker rooms today were nowhere to be found. I think that's one of the reasons that so many guys from that era have a hard time walking down to pick up the mail today. We took our physical vitality for granted.

Not me, not anymore. Cancer has a way of making you focus, but I don't want to see you wait for a cancer diagnosis before you take your body's wellbeing seriously. You can have all the passion in the world and a great plan for building the life of your dreams, but if you feel like forty miles of bad road when you get up in the morning, or you spend half of your time in doctors' offices, you won't achieve much. A low energy level means a low achievement level. If you want to be invincible, be proactive in looking after your body and mind.

# ISOTONIX® PRIME INVINCIBLE HEALTH & WELLNESS FORMULA™

I have to admit it's pretty cool when somebody walks up to me and says, "I can't believe you're 65! What do you do? What do you take?" I chuckle and say that having teenage children keeps you young and so does marrying an athlete. As you know, I still work out, as does Janet. We eat healthy and have been taking our Isotonix® supplements, developed by Market America, for over 15 years … and that's the key to staying young to me. It's no wonder that I've now teamed up with the Science and Product Development teams at Market America, Inc.

They are releasing a new anti-aging dietary supplement specifically formulated for baby boomers, which fits right in with the concept of invincible health and wellness. It is called Isotonix Prime Invincible Health & Wellness Formula. The Isotonix Prime Invincible Health & Wellness Formula is an isotonic-capable product, meaning it has the same fluid pressure as your own body fluids so the formula is rapidly absorbed by the body. There are no binders or fillers and uses the highest quality all-natural ingredients for superior delivery and maximum results. Instead of six hard-to-swallow pills, just one cold, tasty drink will fuel your day.**

When taken with a complete multivitamin and high quality fish oil, Isotonix Prime Invincible Health & Wellness Formula gives you the foundation for an invincible day. It contains select ingredients that work synergistically to support the needs of aging adults. The proprietary formulation contains Branched Chain Amino Acids, FruiteX-B®, Grape Seed Extract and Huperzine A. Isotonix Prime Invincible Health & Wellness Formula helps the aging body retain muscle mass, improves memory and mental focus, supports relief from temporary inflammation associated with the normal aging process and daily activity, contributes to joint comfort, supports a healthy heart, and boosts energy.**

Janet, who has a compromised immune system because she lost her spleen, takes it daily. The isotonic formulation is the best delivery system for her as she, like many, has issues when taking capsules or pills. **Find out more about Isotonix Prime Invincible Health & Wellness Formula at www.isotonix.com.**

## PHYSICALLY INVINCIBLE

Don't get me wrong. You're going to experience some changes in your health as you age. It happens. But changes are all they have to be. I'm 65 at the time of this writing, and I'm in my best shape in years. I run circles around guys in their forties and people regularly think I'm about fifteen years younger than I am. But that hasn't happened by accident.

After colon cancer, my diet changed. No more steak and eggs for me. Now I eat very little red meat. I eat tons of vegetables and fruit. I eat lots of omega 3 fatty acids. I take heart healthy vitamins and magnesium to keep my blood pressure in the healthy range. Because of all the positive changes, my blood pressure, which was borderline, is perfect. My cholesterol has dropped. I have an addiction to chocolate, and I satisfy it with caramel protein bars. I'm very careful about what I eat, because you truly are what you put in your body.

### JANET'S WORDS FOR WOMEN

*One word: SWEAT. Women should not be afraid of muscle. You should love muscle. Muscle defies gravity as you age. When you sweat and work your body, everything is better. Your health is better. Your sex is better. Your self-esteem is better. You feel better about who you are and how you look. Your body is the one thing you can control, even if everything else is going haywire. Exercise kicks in your hormones and adrenaline and relieves stress. It grounds you and makes you feel great. Don't be afraid to work out and work out hard.*

Good health begins in the kitchen. If I could give you three pieces of dietary advice, I would suggest first that you cut out anything white. White flour, white sugar, white bread, white potatoes, white rice. White foods tend to be heavily processed, empty carbs that don't do much for your body. Second, cook at home more. When you eat out, you don't have as much control over your food and it's easy to take in a lot more sodium, fat and calories than you realize. If you doubt me, check out the menu at a restaurant like P.F. Chang's, which lists calories and sodium next to each dish. Believe me, it will make your eyes pop!

# INVINCIBLE MOMENT

When CJ Scarlet's doctor told her in 2002 that her debilitating, long-term autoimmune conditions (lupus and scleroderma) had caused her to develop a progressive heart and lung condition, her life came to a screeching halt. Desperately ill, she struggled to make the best of her remaining time, but fear and misery overrode her attempts to be happy.

One day she had the opportunity to meet with a Tibetan Buddhist lama. She poured out her tale of woe, expecting to receive sympathy. That's when she learned that lamas don't do dramas. Instead, the Lama ordered her to stop feeling sorry for herself and focus her attention on others' happiness. Bored but curious, CJ began actively helping others by performing small acts of kindness. She noticed that when she helped someone, she felt a flush of happiness, so she began to do larger things, like giving her cane to a woman who was struggling to walk and volunteering at the Red Cross after Hurricane Katrina.

Amazingly, the happier she became, the better she felt! Within 18 months, CJ's condition went into remission and she now feels better than she has in twenty years!? Today, CJ Scarlet is an author, motivational speaker, Chief Rover of Roving Coach International, and founder of the Kindness Cure Campaign and The Healing Tree Foundation. She has appeared on numerous radio and television programs, and her first book, Neptune's Gift: Discovering Your Inner Ocean, is now available. She was recently named one of the "Happy 100" people on the planet, and is featured in the new bestseller, Happy for No Reason, by Chicken Soup for the Soul author Marci Shimoff.

Finally, eat more whole food.  Fruit, vegetables, seeds, nuts—it's all great for you and it hasn't been processed at all.  Whole food is packed with nutrients that science doesn't even know about yet, and you won't find them in a vitamin.  Get used to the taste of real food without sweeteners, salt or preservatives.  Trust me, give it some time and your taste buds will adjust…and thank you.

## Q:  What are you putting in your body and how does it make you feel?

**A:** _____

_____

The other must is exercise, and I don't mean playing eighteen holes on the local municipal golf course!  Back in the day when I worked for U.S. Healthcare, I was a personal trainer for many of their executives. Let me tell you, I worked those men and women hard, but it paid off.  They lost weight, medical costs went down, and productivity went up. The Swedes have known this for years: you get more done at work when you are fit, healthy and alert.

Being physically invincible won't solve all your problems.  If you've been afraid to leave your job and start that business, been performing poorly at work or have a bad relationship with your kids, getting fit and healthy isn't a cure-all.  But fitness and health are a foundation for the other positive steps you're going to take, like having a plan and working your guts out.  When you start making radical changes to your life, you're going to need stamina and alertness and a good immune system to fight off the effects of stress. Taking care of your body and mind gives you those gifts.

## VINCE'S FITNESS PRESCRIPTION

You'll want to find a fitness program that works for you and that you enjoy, and you'll want to consult your physician before beginning any exercise regimen. But if you don't know where to start, here's the plan that I follow that gives me, and Janet, great results. Use it if you like, adapt it if you want to, and most important, start slow and find a routine that you can stick with and that gives you variety. The more you surprise your body, the better your results will be.

# INVINCIBLE CIRCUIT FITNESS PROGRAM

- Start your workout with a warm-up, then go into your cardio-vascular work. Take about 15-20 minutes to get up to your target heart rate. Janet and I have five different sets that we do on a universal gym, a Stairmaster, an elliptical machine, a treadmill, dumbbells, and bands.

- After you have done a minimum of 20 minutes of cardio at your target heart rate transition into resistance work with weights, bands or body- weight exercises like pushups or pull-ups. Ideally, use a lower weight with more repetitions so that you can repeat the moves as fast as possible with good form. I am for 20-25 reps of a weight you can handle but gives you good resistance. That keeps the heart rate up—it shouldn't fall below 120. When you do the resistance phase pick two exercises that have the opposite reaction or body part, like a push then a pull exercise, or an upper body then a lower body exercise.

**Here's a simple sample Invincible Circuit for you:**
- 20 minutes of cardio at target heart rate (THR)
- Stretch
- 2 minutes of cardio to get to THR
- 20 reps of lat pull downs followed by 20 reps of bench press
- 2 minutes of cardio to get THR
- 20 reps of curls followed by 20 reps of triceps extension
- 2 minutes of cardio to get to THR
- 20 reps of leg extension followed by 20 reps of leg curls
- 2 minutes of cardio to get to THR
- 20 reps of rowing followed by 20 reps of overhead press
- 2 minutes of cardio to get to THR
- 25 crunches (stomach) rest for 30 seconds and do 25 more crunches
- You can do this circuit again if you wish or improvise with your exercises
- One full circuit like this should take about 50 minutes.
- Once you're done, make sure you cool down with some light cardio moves and stretching, so you don't hurt yourself.
- The key here is consistency and doing this program at least 3 days a week. On the non circuit days do some form of cardio or simply walk for an hour. Don't feel guilty if you miss a workout but try not to miss too many. The results will be amazing if you just stick with the program.

I'm also big into exercise bands. You can get a set of them for $30 and they're great for someone who doesn't have weights. They're also perfect for working out when you travel. Also, one aspect of health and fitness that is very much neglected is rest. Our culture, especially in business, rewards people who burn the candle not only at both ends but in the middle. But if you're only getting five hours of sleep a night, not only are you probably feeling terrible during the day, but you're harming your body's ability to recover from exercise and increasing your risk of injury.

The other key here is to start slow but be consistent. Too many people, when they start exercising after a long time of not working out, do too much too soon and get hurt. You don't need to run five miles on your first run after quitting smoking! Run to the end of the block and back, for crying out loud. Use some common sense. You didn't get out of shape overnight; you're not going to become a triathlete overnight, either. If you get hurt, you'll quit, and that's the surest way to get nowhere.

However, if you start slow, be consistent and slowly make your workouts more and more challenging. Write down your results, whether it's how many reps you did on the bench press machine or what your time was running that mile. Work out five or six days a week and steadily add weight, increase your run distance, bump up the resistance on the elliptical machine, that sort of thing. Over a few months you'll notice yourself becoming stronger and faster with greater stamina, all without suffering pulled hamstrings, a sore back and all the other rewards of overdoing it.

Exercise consistently and with variety. Eat a diet of whole, natural foods. Take supplements. Get enough sleep. That's my formula for invincibility.

## JANET CANTWELL-PAPALE'S FITNESS PRESCRIPTION

**JANET:** I was a sickly kid until I was eleven years old. So today, if I don't work out, I'm miserable. I spent so many years and worked so hard getting in shape and becoming an athlete that it's part of my essence. When I don't work out, I'm hyper and feel bad. When I do, I'm calm and feel fit and sexy and young. Exercise for me is a wonder drug.

I blew out my knee as a gymnast, so part of exercise for me is about keeping my mobility. I have to work out if I don't want a knee replacement sooner rather than later. I do spin, all kinds of cardio, and weights, especially

116

with my legs. My attitude is the more you keep yourself in shape, the less stress you'll suffer on your joints. That's bound to make you feel better, keep you moving and keep you healthier longer.

## Dennis Franks' Fitness Prescription

**VINCE:** My former NFL teammate and good friend Dennis Franks is a work-out machine these days and looks fantastic. The program that he subscribes to is very similar to the one that Janet and I like. He is highly motivated to stay in shape for several reasons:

- Weight Management – he has lost nearly 60 pounds since his playing days

- Overall Fitness

- Stress Reduction – exercise is a proven stress reducer

- Endurance - exercise helps him maintain a frenetic travel and work schedule

- Living Longer – the mortality rate of retired NFL linemen is very high if they do not lose weight and maintain a high level of fitness

Here's what Dennis has to say about his fitness philosophy: "My philosophy in fitness and exercise is that it is a major component in slowing the aging process and maintaining vitality and quality of life. I exercise five days a week for 60 minutes. Monday, Wednesday and Friday I do a cardio body fitness effort for 45 minutes—walk/jog, elliptical, or treadmill. Tuesdays and Thursdays are my personal training days—30 minutes of cardio resistance and stretching. On weekends I do the 'honey do' list and or travel. Its fun, its a habit and has worked for me."

Dennis prefers to work with a trainer a couple of days a week and his program was deigned by Jason Davis in Greensboro, NC.

## Health Leads to Greater Things

The thing I've learned about really being physically and mentally vital is that when you are, your priorities change. Being diagnosed with cancer has changed my life for the better. For instance, I'm a major proponent of cancer screenings, especially the screenings that are easy and effective: colon, prostate, breast, skin, testicular, ovarian. As soon as you're the recommended age—sooner if you have risk factors like a family history of a certain cancer—do me a favor. Go get screened. Tell 'em Vince sent you. The inconvenience will be well worth the peace of mind if you're cancer-free, or early detection and complete cure if you're not.

Also, develop a good relationship with the important healthcare professionals in your life, starting with a physician who you trust and who listens to you. In this group you can also include a personal trainer, a dietician or nutritionist, a massage therapist, or even a chiropractor if that works for you. These professionals are all here to serve the goal of maximizing your health and vitality, so find good ones and work with them to fine-tune your body until it's a smooth-running machine.

One of the best things that's happened to me since cancer is that I've become a spokesman for colon cancer screening through StopColonCancerNow.com's "Get Your Rear In Gear" program. The movie Invincible has been a huge help in spreading the world about the importance and ease of screenings after age 50. When you get a movie made about you that's number-one at the box office, doors open all over the place. It's given me the platform to talk about screening and to write about it in this book. If I can help save a few lives, that will make everything I achieved on the football field pale in comparison.

Just as important as exercise is the food you put in your body. When you're working out hard, you need plenty of lean, natural, organic protein to fuel muscle repair and growth. One of the companies we trust to provide us with that kind of top-quality meat is Rastelli Foods Group. This family business has been around since 1976, and they're a great source for the finest fish, shellfish, poultry, pork, healthy grass-fed beef and much more. We won't get our meat from anybody else.

Find out more about Rastelli Foods Group and their incredible selection of top-quality products at **www.vincepapale.com.**

## END ZONE

**Things to think about & do after finishing this chapter**

■ Talk to a trainer about developing or revamping your workout.
■ Take inventory of your weekly diet and see where you need to cut back on junk and add healthy whole foods.
■ Get a physical.
■ If you're over 50 and haven't been screened, schedule a colonoscopy.
■ Find workout buddies to keep you motivated.

**What's your workout program today and how do you think you could make it more effective?**

_____

_____

_____

_____

_____

_____

_____

_____

_____

_____

_____

_____

_____

_____

_____

_____

# CHAPTER TWELVE

# GO THE EXTRA DEGREE

*"Opportunity is missed by most people because it is dressed in overalls and looks like work."*

— Thomas Edison

A while back I gave a speech in Scottsdale, Arizona for Olympus, the camera company. The theme was, "Go the Extra Degree." When water is heated to 211 degrees Fahrenheit, what happens to it? It gets hot. It might bubble a little, but that's about it. But when you add that extra degree and take it to 212, suddenly it boils. Boiling water produces steam, and steam is energy that can make electricity or power a locomotive. Steam is power and with power you can do anything. Adding that one extra degree can make all the difference between winning and losing.

When I was with the Eagles, Coach Vermeil had many slogans on the locker room walls. One of them said, "Make second effort a part of your personality." Basically, he meant that what is an add-on for other people, something they give only under special circumstances, should really be part of our "first effort." He wanted us not only to be physically tough but mentally tough, to have that never-say-die attitude. But I don't think that "second effort" really covers it anymore. It's like suggesting that you try, but only if your regular effort doesn't get the job done should you buckle down and give more.

No. Being successful today means giving complete extra effort from the first moment. It means completely outworking the other person from the start. That's what going the extra degree means: when you think you've given all you can, finding a little more within yourself that pushes you over the top. When water is at 211 degrees, it's wasting energy. But when you add that one degree...you find your power. Magic happens.

### JANET'S WORDS FOR WOMEN

*Some women, if a man goes to 212 degrees, feel that they need to go to 213. This is especially true in corporate environments. We want to prove we're as good as any man, or better. But that's not always necessary, and when we do that, sometimes we can burn ourselves out. For instance, when I was coaching I would take it to 215 degrees and wind up in the hospital at the end of the year. I always wanted to do more because I was trained to always go for the "10." On the other hand, some women in relationships these days refuse to go the extra degree. They want to bail out of a marriage as soon as*

*things get a little rocky instead of toughing it out and trying to make*
*things work. Sometimes they don't, and that's fine, but I think it's*
*important to give all you have to what matters. Until you do, you*
*really don't know how much "all you have" is.*

## THE SECRET OF ENDURANCE

You can see this idea in the new thinking about the science behind human
endurance. When you look at some of the greatest endurance athletes in the
world, guys who win Ironman and Ultraman races, you have to wonder how
they do it. Endurance racing is about suffering; the guy or gal who can suffer
more and longer than his or her opponents will usually be the one standing
on the podium wearing a medal. Somehow, these men and women find a
way to keep cycling and running when their bodies are screaming at them to
stop, stop, stop the pain.

**JANET:** For years, the whole mechanism governing endurance has been the
lactate threshold. As a former coach, I know all about lactic acid: the harder
you work the muscles anaerobically, the more lactic acid builds up in them.
Lactic acid causes fatigue, so once it gets to a certain level, you stop being
able to exercise. That was always thought to be the limiting factor in triath-
letes; they would hit their lactate limit and the body would say, "Enough!"
But now there's new thinking that the pain and feeling of exhaustion isn't
about lactate, but about something called a governor system.

Basically (says the theory), the governor's job is to keep you from
doing permanent damage to your body through intense exercise. So when
you're doing a triathlon and the agony comes, that's your body warning you,
"Stop, you're about to really do some harm!" The thing is, the governor is
very conservative, so when it warns you to stop you actually still have some
gas left in your tank—if you can ignore all the panicked signals from your
body and keep pushing. This is why some athletes report that when they
pushed through the screaming of the pain and fatigue, they suddenly found
new reserves of endurance. They were able to give one more degree, and
sometimes it made the difference between finishing and not finishing that
Ironman.

**VINCE:** You really don't know how deep you can go until you go there. But when you are phoning it in at work, you never ever reach the point where you can test yourself. If you never find out what's left in your tank when the fuel light flashes, how will you ever know

what you can really accomplish? Fill that tank with incredibly hard work and give yourself a reserve any time you need it.

## A TENTH OF A SECOND

Do you have any idea of how short a tenth of a second is? It's the time it takes a boxing speed bag to make one full swing forward and back when a pro boxer is working it. That's too-fast-for-the-eye speed. But that tiny amount of time can make all the difference in the world if you're an Olympic sprinter. The margin between a medal and no medal in the Olympic 100-meter dash is usually less than a tenth of a second, down to the hundredths of a second.

That's where the extra degree comes in. It's the extra burst of effort or work that can make all the difference when you're trying to land a job, secure a new customer or sell your house. It's doing five more reps with a weight when your muscles are burning. It's spending another hour research-ing online at 3 a.m. to find the perfect video clip for a presentation. It's going above and beyond the call of duty and working a little harder than the next guy. Everything in life is competitive, and if you want to come out on top you need to be the one who's setting the tone and the pace.

The tricky part is that you never know how much extra effort is enough. Unlike water, where you know that one degree from 211 to 212 will make all the difference, you can't really know what it will take to push you over the top. Life doesn't usually come with rules or a map, so if you're trying to figure out how much extra work you need to put in to be great, good luck. Fortunately, there's a solution:

### *Always go the extra degree, no matter what.*

How? There are two ways to go about it. First, you can look at the typical effort that other colleagues, players or friends are putting in and set the bar higher for yourself. Or you can listen to that inner voice that says, "Okay, that's enough for today," and tell it to get lost. There's a part of us that always wants to say, "Stop." But if you can override it and automatically give 5% or 10% more, you'll always be the one working late, pounding out the extra miles or taking the extra steps to keep the customer satisfied. You never have to worry, "How much is enough?" when you're always giving extra.

## INVINCIBLE MOMENTS

*My cousin Cindy Papale shares her own Invincible Moment:*

*"My Invincible Moment began when I got breast cancer. I never thought I could say it, but since I had cancer, life has brought me on an incredible journey of meeting people, some of whom are breast cancer survivors. I've become an advocate and found out that I really enjoy speaking. One of those speaking engagements I'll always remember. It was 2007, and I was speaking to a group of girls from six to 18 years old from the Honeyshine Mentoring Program, an organization for girls in the foster care program sponsored by Tracy Mourning, wife of the NBA star Alonzo Mourning.*

*"One of the little girls, who was maybe eight, asked me, 'How did it feel to wake up not having any breasts?' It was an incredible question; most kids would ask me if I was scared and things like that. I thought about it for a few seconds and then I whipped the question around and turned it into something positive. I told her that when I woke up, I thought I still had breasts because the bandages were so high. I told her that I saw my doctor, took the appropriate medicines, and that's why I'm here today.*

*"I told her that since I had been diagnosed, I had enjoyed the honor of speaking to women and reminding them to do self-exams and that I had met some wonderful people. After I answered, she came up and gave me the best hug and told me I was the bravest person she*

*had ever met. Later, I learned that this little girl had already been in four foster homes. I was truly touched that someone so young would ever think about asking this kind of question.*

*"I always say that we breast cancer survivors are like teabags: You really don't now how strong we are until you put us in hot water. I've found out how strong I am, and I love being able to inspire others like this little girl."*

## REASONS FOR HOLDING BACK

JANET: A lot of athletes aren't successful because they won't put in the extra work. They think they can breeze through on pure talent, and while that might work at the college level, it's different in the pros. If you don't put in the work, you won't stick around.

The thing is, everybody in every profession from sports to sales to teaching knows what it takes to get really good at something, but some just choose not to do it. They would rather be mediocre than pay the price to be great. I guess that's their decision to make, but why would you ever choose to be less than you can be? I couldn't do that even if I wanted to. I'm too driven. But I understand some of the reasons people choose not to go that extra degree:

- **Entitlement.** Some people feel like the world owes them success and they shouldn't have to work too hard to get it. Well, the world owes you exactly nothing. Anyone who wants more needs to work more. A sense of entitlement will get you nowhere. Even legacy admissions to Ivy League schools have to work their butts off eventually, because family connections will only take you so far.

- **Fear of failure.** So you go the extra degree to be successful and you fall flat anyway. So what? Everybody fails. It's trying that makes you a success in the end. Extra work doesn't guarantee you anything; it just improves the odds that you'll get the job, land the client or win the race. But if you're afraid to give that final, small, exhausting push of extra effort, then why bother trying at all?

125

- **They don't believe it will make any difference.** The cynics in the audience may feel like the game is rigged and that no matter how hard they work, the people with the right connections or the talented brown-nosers will get the opportunities. Sure, that can be true sometimes. But I also know that most of the time, hard work and dedication win out. Most people, even the ones sitting in the seats of power, are impressed and moved by tireless hard work and extra effort. They're usually the type of people who go the extra degree themselves; that's how they got to the top. So they appreciate people who do the same.

- **They've been burned.** It's possible that you'll stay up all night to finish that proposal and have someone else take credit for it. You might work for weeks to finish your book manuscript ahead of schedule only to have an editor reject it. Get over it. It happens. Sometimes, no good deed goes unpunished. But the alternative is to cower and assume that no matter what you do, it's never going to be good enough. Remember, the Harry Potter books were rejected by nine publishers before Bloomsbury bought them and made them a worldwide sensation. "Keep trying" is the only success advice that never fails.

## KEEP YOURSELF FRESH

**VINCE:** Remember, some people will resent you for putting in extra effort and going the extra degree because it makes them look bad. Nobody who's habitually lazy wants his laziness exposed. But that's their problem, not yours. If someone accuses you of making the team look bad, tell them they should step up their game.

Constantly going that extra degree is the best way to keep yourself fresh and excited about what you do. It gets great results. It shows you new capabilities you

> **INVINCIBLE WISDOM**
>
> *"It is only through labor and painful effort, by grim energy and resolute courage, that we move on to better things."*
>
> — *Theodore Roosevelt*

might not know you have. It brings new opportunities that keep your zest for life fresh. I'm 65, and when I go to charity events I see people much younger than me who look ten years older. They look like they're done with living. They look and act old. Age is an attitude and you're only as old as you feel. Right now I feel great. We were made to strive and overcome. It brings out the best in us and the people who help and care about us. If you take only one thing away from this book, take that.

## END ZONE

**Things to think about & do after finishing this chapter**

- Look at the ways you could go the extra degree in your work, fitness or relationships.
- Figure out what's stopped you from doing that in the past. Was it fear, laziness or the feeling that it just didn't make any difference?
- Plan out the ways you'll make extra effort a normal part of your approach to things—figure out the typical level of work that people do in your field and add 10%.
- Map out the goals you could achieve with that extra 10%. Would it mean the difference between running a half-marathon and a marathon? Making $75,000 next year and making $125,000?

**What do you fear most?**

_____

_____

_____

**What will you do to overcome that fear?**

_____

_____

_____

**What can you do to get that extra degree?**

_____

_____

_____

# CHAPTER THIRTEEN

# FORGET YOUR WEAKNESSES, WORK ON YOUR STRENGTHS

*"We gain strength, and courage, and confidence by each experience in which we really stop to look fear in the face… we must do that which we think we cannot."*

— Eleanor Roosevelt

When I was trying to make the Eagles, I knew the deck was stacked against me. In a traditional training camp, I wouldn't have stood a chance. First, I was too old at 30. No team that's trying to build for the long term would invest a roster spot in a guy my age who had never played college ball. By their logic, I might have at most a five-year career. I would be more likely to get injured than a 22-year-old. And I would be taking a roster spot away from a young kid out of Ohio State or USC who might become the cornerstone of the team for a decade. All those views are valid.

The lucky thing for me was that Coach Vermeil wasn't running a traditional camp. He was rebuilding from the ground up based in large part on character, guts and work ethic—and I thought I had a decent chance to compete in those areas. Still, the cards were stacked against me. I didn't have college experience. I had very little experience as a wide receiver. Despite my raw speed, the little nuances of football that were unconscious and second nature to the other guys were an effort for me because I hadn't been playing nonstop since I was eight years old. I realized that I couldn't do anything about those shortcomings. I could only focus on what I did well.

So that's what I did. My strengths were that I was one of the fastest guys in camp, I could catch the football, and I didn't mind hitting and getting hit. I also liked to work hard and I had great concentration and the ability to focus on the simple things. So I set about making my strengths even stronger and didn't worry about my weaknesses. I worked extra hard in drills. I made sure to show off my speed every chance I got. I learned everything I could about the finer points of catching a football. I went out of my way to lay blistering blocks and tackles on other guys. I highlighted what I did well and hoped that it would make up for all the things I couldn't do well.

Obviously, it worked out just fine.

## WHAT COULD YOU BE GREAT AT?

**JANET:** As Jim Collins wrote in his bestseller *Good to Great*, good is the enemy of great. Some people are good at a lot of things but never become great at anything because they're afraid to fail. Sometimes, you have to choose. If you have a child who's good at football, basketball and guitar, eventually you're going to have to help that child choose which to follow—and you could make the wrong choice.

That's the risk you have to accept, because the alternative is trying to do everything so that you're good at a bunch of things but miss out on greatness. You have to balance your dreams with what you're truly gifted at. We always want to do what doesn't come naturally. People who can't sing want to sing. People who can't paint—even though they might be terrific at ten other things—want desperately to paint. It's human nature. But you have to look at your gifts honestly so you don't waste them.

That's what's great about being young: you can experiment. If you've always dreamed about being something, even if no one believed in you, you can try for a few years. If it doesn't work out, you can try something else. That's what I did. Nobody believed I could be a gymnast, but I had the freedom to try. Greatness is too precious to let go without at least trying.

## CATCH YOURSELF DOING SOMETHING RIGHT

VINCE: Many people think that life is all about competition with others, and sometimes that's true. But in reality, your biggest competition is yourself. It's you versus you. The trouble is, when you look at the ways you can make more money or get that promotion, you're probably taking aim at your weak spots. Maybe you're not a good public speaker. Maybe you don't grasp technology as intuitively as some younger people who grew up with it. Maybe you're not the most organized person. Whatever your roster of weaknesses is, do you list them and make a plan to fix them, like you're a contractor repairing problems in an old house?

That's the wrong way to go about getting what you want. Look, I'm not saying that you shouldn't work on improving yourself. Of course you should. If you don't speak well, then by all means join Toastmasters and learn. If you take too many sick days because you're overweight and your diet stinks, start working out and eating right. But if you really want to get ahead—if you really want to be invincible—then focus on making your strengths even stronger. Shore up your weaknesses, but make getting better at what you're already good at your top priority.

There are some really sound reasons for doing this:

- **You're ahead of the pack.** Let's say you're a professional vocalist and you want to get more gigs and more recognition. But instead of becoming a better singer, you decide to do it by learning the blues harmonica, which you've barely played. You figure learning the harp will make you stand out. But you're being compared with musicians who've been blowing harmonica for 40 years, and against them you sound terrible. When you try to strengthen a weakness, you start the race far behind. If it's your passion, give it a try, but don't expect to be proficient very quickly. On the other hand, when you refine and polish skills that are already at a high level, you gain ground on everyone else. Being among the best in your field is a great way to grab opportunities.

- **You get to enjoy some success.** I'm not saying you shouldn't learn new things; it's a great way to keep yourself fresh and challenged. But while you're at it, why not also take classes or training in what you're great at? That way, you get to catch yourself doing something well. You get to feel good about your talents. Attending a master class in marketing or learning how to design better apps for the iPhone leverages your existing skill set, lets you show off a little, and gives you quick success, which boosts your morale and fuels even more learning.

- **People already know you for these things.** Don't reinvent the wheel. Unless you are completely ready to ditch your current vocation and do something completely different, then it's a waste of your time to work on an area where you're not already known for being highly skilled. Executives, clients, media—they know you as X, and they know you're good. To retrain them to think of you as Y is a long arduous process, during which other people are probably grabbing opportunities that should have been yours.

- **You'll progress faster.** Nobody likes to struggle. We all want to learn fast and get better. That's not going to happen if you're taking training in something you've never done before. But when you take a gifted leader and put her in a seminar where she learns even more advanced leadership skills, she's probably going to gain proficiency with lightning speed. There's nothing bad about that.

## SOMETIMES, STRENGTH IS IGNORING YOUR WEAKNESSES

As I've said, I do a lot of work with the Paralyzed Veterans Association. While working on this book, I went to Walter Reed Hospital to meet some of these veterans and I was absolutely amazed by their heart and courage. There's a reason we call these men and women "Wounded Warriors." They are my heroes. They come in all sizes, shapes, sexes, races, and religions. They are undrafted free agents who signed on to protect the American Dream and were given no signing bonuses, no press conferences and no guarantees. They wore (and still wear) their uniforms with pride. There are no corporate logos on them, just medals & stripes earned through sweat and blood.

### JANET'S WORDS FOR WOMEN

*Write down what you're good at. If you don't know, start with the basics. Are you a good listener? Are people able to talk to you? Are you a problem solver? If you're great at something, celebrate it and find a way to incorporate it in what you do. It's all right to admit you're the cream of the crop at something, because someday, you won't be.*

There's no sense of entitlement. These vets risked their lives every day to make sure our dreams were protected, and in the end their own bodies were shattered. They are looking for a second chance in life. I went to meet them to try to inspire them, but I came away inspired myself, blown away by courage and attitudes that I have never seen before. They have lost limbs and organs, true. But what could never be taken away from these warriors is their heart. Each one beats as strongly as ever as they bust their butts everyday to get back into life.

Back when I was playing, our Special Teams Coach Ken Iman gave out what was called the "Who's Nuts?" Award. It went to the guy who played with the most guts and fury that week—basically, the player who said, "Screw the limits." I was proud to win it

*Who's Nuts Baby? These tee-shirts were coveted my Special Teamers ... a reward for making a game changing play on the Special Teams.*

more than once. Well, my "Who's Nuts" Award forever goes to the warriors I have met from the PVA. They have shown me what it's like to be really invincible. A huge part of that is ignoring what they don't have anymore. Think about it. Before you went to Iraq or Afghanistan, you dreamed of becoming a cop or a truck driver or climbing Mount Everest (like the guy in our Invincible Moments story in this chapter). Then an IED took both your legs and that dream is gone. Forever. Who in his or her right mind wouldn't dwell on that loss?

Only these vets don't...or if they do, they don't show it. They focus on what they can do, not what they can't. They will their shattered bodies to do things that most of us couldn't do. They are proof that the mind is an incredible thing; it can make you do things that you never thought you could. For them, every day is an Invincible Moment.

Sometimes, strength is looking past your weakness and accepting that you'll never be a published novelist, a pro baseball player or a Congresswoman and moving on to what you can do. It's doing instead of grieving for what's lost or impossible. It takes incredible courage to face life as it is, not as we wish it could be. That's how we make it better.

# INVINCIBLE MOMENTS

Fitness trainer and extreme adventurer Sean Burch shares his high-altitude Invincible Moment:

"I was in my twenties, and I had dreamt about climbing Everest for about eight years. Then I got a job, bought a house with a white picket fence, and thought, 'Is this all there is?' I was fascinated with mountain climbers but it had never occurred to me to actually do what they did.

"Then my grandfather got sick. He was 86 and had done everything: been in World War II, traveled all over the globe and more. He was a tough Norwegian and used to walk six miles a day and was sad that he could no longer do what he'd been used to, but his mind was clear. He said to me, 'You've got to live your life. There are so many things I have not done.' I said that as far as I was concerned, he'd done everything. He squeezed my hand and practically screamed, "'No, there is so much more! You must live your life!' We thought he was losing it, and he slipped back into a comatose state.

"But a few weeks later I thought about what he had said. Was I going to go through the motions in my life—have a house, get married and then look back on what I had missed? I had my Invincible Moment then and there. I decided that I was going to live my life the way my grandfather did: fully, doing everything. I was going to climb Mount Everest.

"Predictably, everyone thought I was crazy. I lived in Washington, DC. There were no mountains nearby. I was 29 with no experience. But I decided I would learn and climb the way an honorable person did it: just me and the mountain. I spent four years training, and in 2003 I climbed Everest solo.

"That was only the beginning. I went to the North Pole and ran a marathon there. I wrote and published a book in 2007. I hold multiple Guinness records for fastest summits of several major mountains, including 23 unclimbed Himalayan peaks. I've remade my life as an extreme adventurer and someone who trains others to be fit enough to climb their personal Everests.

*"When you do what I do, you have many moments when you really grow, when life is laid bare. Those are the moments I cherish. I had one of those moments when I was climbing Everest. It was 9:30 at night and I was in my tent alone, freezing. I had to ask myself, 'No one is going to save you. Are you going to die or are you going to live?' Since then I try to live every moment as though it's my last and to help carry others along the way."*

## DO YOU NEED A LIFE COACH?

**JANET:** Everybody has strengths and gifts. You just have to be honest with yourself about what you can and can't do. After my knee injury, it was incredibly hard for me to admit to myself that I wasn't going to be able to perform as a gymnast at the level I had before. That's the risk you take in any sport; the wrong kind of injury can finish you. I was able to look honestly at my situation and move on, but it took time to heal emotionally and physically.

If you can't do that, maybe you need a life coach. If it's really difficult for you to assess your own strengths and weaknesses, it's a great idea to find an objective person who's trained and experienced to help you break through and see yourself clearly.

A good life coach will be trained (and maybe even certified by a body like the International Coach Federation) to help people discover their aptitudes (what they're good at), attitudes (their patterns of thinking, positive and negative), and altitudes (their dreams and aspirations for life). He or she guides, encourages, reveals and occasionally delivers well-placed kicks to the backside to get you to see things clearly and make decisions that serve your long-term purpose.

Believe me, it's no sign of weakness to hire a life coach. Some of the most successful people in the world have them. They know that sometimes the best sign of strength is the ability to admit that you're weak and ask for help. They know that being intellectually brilliant or artistically gifted doesn't mean you can get out of your own way. If you can't afford a coach, find a mentor. For some people, the best way to avoid becoming lazy and distracted is to make themselves accountable to someone else.

> ## NVINCIBLE WISDOM
>
> *"I love the man that can smile in trouble, that can gather strength from distress, and grow brave by reflection."*
>
> — *Thomas Paine*

**VINCE:** One final word: we're not against working on your weaknesses and trying new things. That would be ridiculous. What would life be if we stopped stepping out into thin air without a net and attempting something that we've never done before? All Janet and I are saying is that you shouldn't define yourself by what you can't do, but by what you can do and what you have the courage to try. Don't obsess over your weaknesses or feel bad about them. If you choose, invest some time trying to turn them into strengths. If you can't, at least you tried. But never forget that in some areas, you're already a genius.

## ND ZONE

**Things to think about & do after finishing this chapter**

- Seek out three people who will honestly assess your strengths and weaknesses.
- Spend some time and analyze how your strengths have contributed to where you are in your life or career. Do the same in figuring out how your weaknesses may have held you back.
- Research life coaches and if you're intrigued, check one out personally.
- Ask your boss, teacher or other superior how you could build on one of your strengths to improve your opportunities or your progress toward your goals.

## INVINCIBLE SELF-ASSESSMENT

### MY STRENGTHS AND WEAKNESSES

**1. My strengths according to me:**

_____

_____

_____

**2. My strengths according to 3 people I trust:**

_____

_____

_____

**3. My weaknesses, according to me:**

_____

_____

_____

**4. My weaknesses, according to 3 people I trust:**

_____

_____

_____

**5. What I can do to improve on my strengths:**

_____

_____

**6. 3 practical steps to make that happen:**

_____

_____

_____

**7. Is it worth my time to shore up my weak spots?**

_____

_____

**8. If yes, what are 3 practical ways I could make that happen?**

_____

_____

_____

**9. 3 ways that a professional life coach could help me:**

_____

_____

_____

# CHAPTER FOURTEEN

# NEGATIVES
# ARE FOR DARKROOMS

"A pessimist sees the difficulty in every
opportunity; an optimist sees the opportunity
in every difficulty."

— Winston Churchill

You've heard the saying, "If it bleeds, it leads," right? Let me tell you, that is 100% true. For a few years after I left football I worked as a sportscaster, and when I was in the newsroom the stories that got far and away the most attention were the negative ones. The scarier and bloodier they were, the better the program director and news anchors liked it. A local teacher wins a national Teacher of the Year award? Yawn. But one incident of a guy breaking into a local home and swiping a toaster oven and there's full 24-hour coverage of the Home Invasion Panic. The news people would make inappropriate cracks about terrible stories because they had become so desensitized to them.

It's the same in national media, or worse. Frightening, negative, shocking stories get ratings, sell products and keep people interested. It's no wonder that we take such a negative view of the world. In a June 2011 poll, 58% of Americans believed the country was headed in the wrong direction. Never mind that many people's idea of the wrong direction is completely different; many of us just feel bad things are happening no matter who's president or who's in control of Congress. Negative sells and our society feeds it to us.

It's easy when things are so difficult economically. There's a lot of pain out there. Most of us know someone who's lost his or her job and maybe his or her house. People are scared. Their way of life seems to be vanishing before their eyes and they don't know what to do about it. When there's high unemployment, freak storms, flooding rivers and gridlock in Washington, it's hard to keep a positive attitude.

But you've got to train yourself to look at the positive and ignore our obsession with the negative, the ugly, the spiteful and the cynical. There's a lot more hope than we realize, but you can't see it if you let your mind dwell only on what's wrong.

**JANET:** You've really got to make a conscious effort to be positive. I had a friend who used to slap himself in the face every morning and say, "You sexy son of a bitch, you're going to have a great day!" You have to love that. Some people can look at the world and see what they need to do. I tend to jump in and make things happen. If you fail, you fail. If that happens, you can go back to what you know so that you're not lost.

## JANET'S WORDS FOR WOMEN

*Take pictures of the good things you want to happen. Cut things out
of magazines. Stay focused. Imagine something positive happening in
the future. Women tend to be harder on ourselves than men are. We
have a lot of negative messages coming at us. We see a wrinkle and
say, "Oh my God!" When you need to stay positive, work harder.
Start trying things outside the box. Ask questions of other people and
find out how they made something good happen. You might be surprised that what you want is not as hard as it appears.*

## IT WAS ALL ON ME

**VINCE:** After my career ended in 1979, I had a tough time being out of
football, even though the whole thing had been a Cinderella story from
the beginning. I should have been happy and grateful, but instead it was
hard for me to stay positive about my life going forward. I did a self-assess-
ment, but it was incomplete. I tried to coach myself but I really wasn't
emotionally mature enough to make that work.

I got professional help. People had been telling me for years I was
crazy, so I finally said, "What the hell, I'll see a shrink." It turned out to be
one of the most positive steps I've ever taken. Seeing a therapist helped
me understand my more emotionally underdeveloped side, the part that
had always given me such a hard time in relationships and put me on such
an emotional roller coaster. The experience not only helped me put a positive spin on my post-football life, it made me understand something really
important:

### *Being positive or negative is a choice and a habit.*

We tend to think that the way we see the world when we wake up in
the morning is what we're stuck with for the entire day. But it's not. You
might start the day set on feeling like everything is turning to crap, but you
don't have to stay that way. You have the power to re-orient your attitude if
you choose to. Positive or negative thinking is a habit, and habits can be

changed. It's not easy—it takes time and constant reminders to keep from lapsing back into the old way of doing things—but it can be done. I did it. So have all of the most successful people in the world. You won't find a pessimist among them, because positive thinking is one of the few ironclad must-haves for any sort of success in life.

> ### INVINCIBLE WISDOM
>
> *"There is little difference in people, but that little difference makes a big difference. The little difference is attitude. The big difference is whether it is positive or negative."*
>
> — W. Clement Stone

I'm serious. Look at me. I was an NFL player for three years and change, but I've been something else for more than 30 years since then. All the success I enjoy today in my marriage to Janet, my fantastic kids, my speaking career, the *Invincible* movie and all the rest has come since I learned to control my emotions and consciously turn myself into a positive, life affirming person. If I was a downer, convinced that I couldn't do this or that or that the world was a lousy place, no one would want me to speak at their events. I wouldn't have all the fantastic friends from my playing days like Denny Franks and Ron Jaworski. No one wants to be around a constantly negative, self-defeating person.

You think my beating cancer was an accident? No way. I had great doctors, great timing in catching it early (thanks to Janet's persistence), and I was in good physical health, which helped my recovery. But I also had a positive attitude. At first, I was scared and feeling down, but Janet snapped me out of it and reminded me that I could beat the disease—and as usual, she was right. I chose to be positive. Nobody else but you has that ability. You're the only one who can make the deliberate decision to see the events of your life in a beneficial, empowering way. And believe me, if I can do it, anybody can.

## DOES THINKING POSITIVE CHANGE ANYTHING?

**JANET:** We don't do New Age around here. We're not going to tell you all about how your thinking can change the world and bring you whatever you want. That's not how life works. However, how you think does change your approach to the world, and that makes all the difference. So yes, positive thinking does change things.

The one thing none of us can afford is to be in denial, and there's a thin line between positive thinking and denial of reality. There's also a thin line between admitting reality and being negative about it. The difference comes in how you think about the reality that's in front of you. Like in gymnastics, it's largely about balance. You have to strike a balance between looking honestly at the reality of your situation, not denying that it exists, but also not being defeated by the challenge you face. It looks something like this:

*Denial_____Empowerment_____Defeat*

At one extreme, you refuse to admit what's happening because, deep down, you're afraid you don't have the guts or ability to rise above it. On the other, you admit it but immediately say, "I can't handle it. It's too much for me." But the key word is in the middle: Empowerment. Balancing realistic thinking with positive thinking empowers you. It's like you're giving yourself permission to be a grownup. For instance, when my knee injury ended my gymnastics career, I could have chosen

to dwell on what I'd lost and be depressed. I could have chosen to deny what had happened and spend years trying to get back to an elite level that my body would no longer allow. Instead, I chose to empower myself. I found diving and excelled at that, and then I became one hell of a coach. I said, "Yes, this has happened and these are the limits that I face, and I choose to

*Janet re-invented herself from a world class gymnast to a record setting diver at Penn State University where she set all of their diving records. Here she is performing a front 2 1/2 off the 3 meter diving board.*

overcome them." That's empowerment.

Thinking positive doesn't mean closing your eyes, sticking your fingers in your ears and singing "La la la" when things are going horribly. It means acknowledging reality but granting yourself the strength and will to create a good outcome. Positive thinking opens doors; negative thinking slams them shut. If you empower yourself, you can turn almost any crisis in life—a job loss, an illness, a breakup—into a blessing that makes you stronger, wiser and happier. Believe me, I've done it.

## INVINCIBLE MOMENT

*Janet shares her own Invincible Moment:*

*"When I was nine years old, I was in a sledding accident. My friend and I hit a tree. She scraped her knee and couldn't walk, so I pulled her home on the sled. I was a tough girl, because what I didn't know at the time was that I had ruptured my spleen. When I got home, my family rushed me to the hospital. I was in such bad shape that a priest gave me last rites. Later, I had emergency surgery to remove my spleen, which saved my life but left me taking a daily dose of penicillin until I was 20.*

*"After that, I was just the sickly girl with no immune system. I remember going into the gym and nobody wanted anything to do with me. I pleaded with my family to let me do gymnastics, and they said, 'We can't send you to gymnastics, you're never going to be able to do anything.'*

*"I said, 'You're never going to say that to me again.' That was my Invincible Moment. I became the most determined kid in gymnastics. I wanted to prove everyone wrong, and I did. When I was a gymnastics coach at Penn, I always tried to recruit the kids who hadn't reached their potential—who had something more to give. They reminded me of myself."*

## RUDY AND EDDIE

**VINCE:** Janet's never-say-die moxie is one of the reasons I married her, and she's got it absolutely right. Positive thinking is a goal in itself, because it actually inspires people. One of the best examples I know is a guy I talk about in a lot of my speeches, Daniel "Rudy" Ruettiger, the subject of the hit movie, *Rudy*.

You might know the story already. Rudy had always dreamed about going to Notre Dame University and playing football for the Fighting Irish, but he couldn't get in. Plus he was way too small for college football. But he never gave up that dream. He was finally accepted into the university and eventually made it onto the Notre Dame practice team. In 1975, in what would have been his last chance to play for the Irish, the coach actually put him in for two plays against Georgia Tech. On the second, Rudy sacked the quarterback, and his teammates carried him off the field.

That's the power of relentless positive thinking. Sure, Rudy's idea of playing for the Irish was unrealistic, but he wasn't looking for a pro football career. He just wanted to be part of an institution that he loved. Because he never gave up and kept his dream in front of him—and because he took steps to make it happen—other people were inspired to make it come true. To this day, Rudy is a friend of mine with his own foundation and the Rudy Awards, which tries to find a "Rudy"—a player with uncommon heart and drive—on every high school team in America.

Here's another example: Eddie Edwards. Remember "Eddie the Eagle," the British ski jumper at the 1984 Winter Olympics? The near-sighted, pudgy guy with the Coke bottle glasses who finished last in every ski jumping event? Of course you do. But you don't remember him because of his ineptitude (an Italian newspaper called him a "ski dropper"), but because no matter what, he was always smiling. He was happy just to be in the Games and it showed. Everybody loved Eddie, because he wasn't a perfect athletic machine. He was us.

Eddie wound up being the first athlete mentioned by name in the closing ceremonies, became an international celebrity, and wound up carrying the torch in the relay for the 2010 Vancouver Olympics, smiling all the way. Now there's a movie in the works about his life.

Why? In part, it's because he never lost faith and stayed positive through it all. Positive thinking really does make other people smile. It gives them hope and helps remind them that good things can happen.

> INVINCIBLE WISDOM
>
> *"I let negativity roll off me like water off a duck's back. If it's not positive, I didn't hear it."*
>
> — *George Foreman*

## HOW TO STAY POSITIVE

Finding your own inner Rudy isn't hard if you choose to make it happen. Whatever is happening in your life or career, you can elect to see the positive side in it. Maybe it's just that you're going to grow and become smarter. With some events, that's all you can get out of them, but that's no small benefit. What's the point of life if you don't get better at it?

When you're dealing with difficult times and struggling to stay positive about the future, I find it incredibly helpful to be around positive people. Being a speaker helps me feed off the energy of others, and that's a great way to stay positive. If you're trying to shift your habit of thinking negatively, get the people out of your life who are always talking about how bad things are and how helpless they are. That kind of thinking is an excuse for giving up. Surround yourself with people who are hopeful about the future and feel confident about their ability to make good things happen.

**JANET:** Another important thing is not to wallow in what's wrong in your life. If you lost your job, feeling bad about it isn't going to get you another one. Have a good cry or break something if it makes you feel better, then get over it. Consciously move your thinking to the next question: What do I do next? When you're planning your forward motion instead of reliving all the bad things that have happened, you find that you feel a new sense of purpose. You're not depressed or blaming or hopeless.

You can develop a habit of positive thinking by getting out and doing something that takes you in the direction you want your life to go, even if it's something small. Had a bad breakup or divorce? Okay, we've all gone through those. But rather than mope and feel like no one is ever going to love you again, why not go to the gym and get in a great work-out? Once you do, you feel better because you've done something good for your body and you're on your way to looking better, too. Whenever you feel weighed down by negatives in your life, whether they're about money, work, health, relationships or anything else, take action. You'll feel better instantly.

**VINCE:** One more thing that I believe in is getting the full picture. Sometimes you're in a negative place because you don't know everything that's going on. Let's say you hear a layoff rumor at your workplace. If you didn't get more information, you might assume you were on the chopping block and become depressed and angry. But if you talk to your boss, you find out that your job is safe. Get all the facts, and get the perspective of other people on things before you assume the worst. None of us can see everything that's happening. When you have the big picture, sometimes things are a lot better than you thought they were!

# END ZONE

**Things to think about & do after finishing this chapter**

■ Write down the names of the three people who best help you remain positive.

_____

_____

_____

■ Write down the names of the three people who are the most negative influences in your life.

_____

_____

_____

■ How can you increase the influence of the first group and decrease the influence of the second?

_____

_____

_____

**Do you tend to think more positively or negatively?**

_____

_____

**Why?**

_____

_____

**List three things you could do today to change your habits and empower yourself.**

_____

_____

_____

# CHAPTER FIFTEEN

# CELEBRATE THE SMALL VICTORIES

*"There are three things we all should do every day. Number one is laugh. Number two is think. And number three is…have your emotions moved to tears…think about it. If you laugh, you think, and you cry, that's a full day. You do that seven days a week, you're going to have something special."*

— Jim Valvano

That picture of me and my old buddy Denny Franks at the end of this chapter is one of my favorites. Denny has an amazing laugh, one of the best and most infectious I've ever heard, and it sums up for me what life in the NFL was about. Fun. Enjoyment. Living out a dream. The thing was, the Eagles were mostly bad when I played. Occasionally, we were terrible. In 1976 and 1977, our combined record was 9-19, and that was an improvement over the pre-Vermeil days. What was really improving was the team attitude. Even though we were still losing, we were losing close games and we knew we were on the verge of turning the corner. Only in my last year, 1978, did we become a decent team, finishing at 9-7. But while I wanted to win as much as the next guy, I also knew that I was part of something special. I was inspiring an entire city with every game. I was helping Coach Vermeil set a new standard for fitness and hard work. I was living the fantasy of every kid who'd grown up rooting for guys like Tommy Mc Donald, Pete Retzlaf, Tom Brookshier and the 1960 NFL championship team.

Win or lose, I had a great time. Part of it was that I had nothing to lose, because I wasn't supposed to be in the NFL to begin with. But beyond that, I learned to appreciate the little things that didn't depend on us winning: a great tackle, an awesome performance from one of my teammates, a day when my posse of neighborhood crazies screamed my name especially loudly and made me feel like a champ. I learned to value all those small things and not to worry about trying to carry the Eagles to victory all by myself. I didn't have the power to do that, just like you don't have the power to double your company's stock price on your own.

The key to keeping on and staying positive, I discovered, is to celebrate the small things you do right—to bask in the momentary rays of sunshine, even when the clouds are ready to roll right back in. Being kind and generous to yourself is what keeps you going.

## OUTSIDE THE BOX AT PENN

**JANET:** When I got my position at Penn, I still had a year of college to go, and I could only keep the head coaching job if I got my degree. The main problem was that I still had to do my student teaching,

which for Penn was two hours away in Hershey, Pennsylvania. There was
no way I could have done that and kept coaching. I could have done my
teaching at Temple University, but that would have meant going to school
for another two years. I was in a box.

So I thought outside that box. I went to Penn State and asked
them if I paid my tuition and student taught somewhere in Philadelphia or
along the Main Line, and had teachers from Temple observe me, would
that count for my student teaching? They looked at me like I was crazy;
nobody had ever asked for something so outrageous. But they let me do it.

That was a small victory; I celebrated it. Later I took a couple of
correspondence courses. Another celebration. I took some courses at
Penn. Yet another celebration. I went to South Africa and taught teachers to teach…and celebrated that. In one year, I got my degree because I

*The University of Pennsylvania Gymnastics Team. Janet Cantwell, Coach*
*(back row, center)*

got out of the limitations they had put on me. One of the ways I kept myself going was to give myself full credit for each step.

## YOUR BEST IS ALWAYS ENOUGH

**VINCE:** That's a classic Janet story. She wasn't worrying about what anybody else thought; she was just doing what she needed to do. In his bestselling P90X workout series, superstar trainer Tony Horton has a catchphrase that I love: "Do your best and forget the rest." That's great advice. We tell our kids to be the best they can be and not to worry about the other guys. Too many of us don't give ourselves credit for the things we do right because we're too busy beating ourselves up for the smallest of mistakes. This might sound familiar: you're in charge of a big meeting, you put together a great presentation, you provide killer sales figures and market data, you give a fine speech...and two slides go missing from your PowerPoint. After it's all over, what are you focusing on? Chances are while everyone else is congratulating you on a job well done, you're beating yourself up over a small missed detail.

> ### INVINCIBLE WISDOM
>
> *"Victory is won not in miles but in inches. Win a little now, hold your ground, and later, win a little more."*
>
> — *Louis L'Amour*

Why? Do we really expect ourselves to be so perfect that we're not allowed to make any mistakes? Do we fear failure that much? Sometimes, yes. I also think we've internalized this idea that it's improper to pat ourselves on the back and give ourselves credit when we do something well. But there is absolutely nothing wrong with a little cheerleading for yourself and even giving yourself a reward for a job well done. When I made the Eagles and got paid, and I wanted a new stereo, I went out and got it. I figured I had put in a ton of bloody work to get that paycheck and I deserved to enjoy it. When I was first married, I wanted a new mountain bike, so I went out and spent a lot of money on a bike that would last me a while. As a matter of fact, I think it lasted longer than that marriage did.

The thing is, effort matters as much or more than success. When you give your very best, no matter what the result, you always win. Your best is always enough. Unfortunately, we tend to focus only on winners. In his book *I'm Here to Win*, Ironman champion Chris McCormack writes, "People look at results, not races." What he means is that people only care about who finishes first without considering the underlying performance. For example, McCormack talks about how people wrote him off after his 2009 Ironman because he finished fourth, but it was because he had an unusually poor swim leg. If they had been paying attention to the race and not just the results, he says, they would have realized that with an improved swim he would be poised for a big win in 2010—which is exactly what happened.

Vince Lombardi may have said, "Winning isn't everything, it's the only thing," but he also said, "It's easy to have faith in yourself and have discipline when you're a winner, when you're number one. What you got to have is faith and discipline when you're not a winner." You're not going to win all the time, no matter how talented you are or how hard you work. Celebrating your small wins—the good first date, the well-painted room in your new house, finally figuring out how to use your iPad without your kids' help—gives you a morale boost and keeps you working toward the bigger goals. As long as you do your best, you have something to be proud of.

## WHAT TO CELEBRATE

Okay, you shouldn't celebrate out and out losses that hurt everyone. Not getting a big client is in no way a reason for a party. It's also not all right to brag when you are the only one in a group or on a team who makes out well. It's not all right to have your softball team get killed 22-5 but strut around the pizza place after the game pointing at your chest and bellowing, "Four for four, baby!" You don't pop champagne to toast your big raise when the other three people in your department didn't get a pay increase.

There's an etiquette involved in giving yourself praise for the little things. The good and bad of celebrating the small stuff:

- **Good:** You go out to dinner because layoff notices were handed out and you didn't get one.

- **Bad:** You take your three buddies who did get layoff notices…and make them each buy a round.

- **Good:** You're pumped because you managed to run three miles of your five-mile morning run.

- **Bad:** You also tore your hamstring.

- **Good:** Your novel is going nowhere but you sell a short story to a magazine.  You brag on Facebook.

- **Bad:** The story is a thinly veiled parody of your boss.  He sees your Facebook post, reads the story and fires you.

The main idea is to let yourself feel proud and happy about the small wins that show you that you're on your way to something bigger and better.  If you're out to lose 75 pounds, you're not going to accomplish that in any one month, but that's no reason not to go a little nuts if you lose ten pounds in a month.  It's a signpost of progress.  If you apply for a job that you want badly and don't get it, but the boss emails you to tell you that you gave a terrific interview, that's reason to dance a little.  You performed well under pressure and odds are the next time that company has an opening, you'll be the first one they call.

When I was in training camp for the Eagles, we would take any reason to celebrate. The harder you're working, the more important even the tiniest pleasures become.  We would celebrate making it through one of our tough practices.  We would celebrate at night when we didn't have any meetings.  A practice without full pads was practically an excuse for a party.

If you look at celebrating the small victories as an excuse for turning even minor wins into morale-boosting events, then the list of candidates becomes pretty long:

- Making it to the end of a tough week.

- Paying off your credit card.

- Losing five pounds.

- Finishing a long book.

- Getting a good performance review.

- Doing your first Skype call.

- Sending your first tweet.

- Setting an appointment with that tough customer.

If you think about, you can probably come up with a dozen small victories you've experienced just in the last week.  If you didn't take give yourself the pleasure of savoring them at the time, do it now.  Anything you did where you gave your best effort and enjoyed even a small success is worth feeling good about.

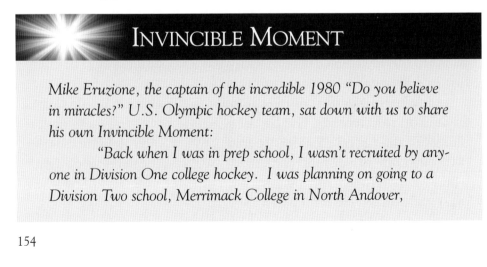

## INVINCIBLE MOMENT

*Mike Eruzione, the captain of the incredible 1980 "Do you believe in miracles?" U.S. Olympic hockey team, sat down with us to share his own Invincible Moment:*
> "Back when I was in prep school, I wasn't recruited by anyone in Division One college hockey.  I was planning on going to a Division Two school, Merrimack College in North Andover,

Massachusetts. It was late August and I was waiting for school to start. I wasn't playing summer hockey, because in summer I was more of a baseball guy. But a buddy called and asked me if I knew anyone who could play in a game, and I volunteered.

"So we played the game and I played hard and very well. The referee was a guy named Jack Parker. Little did I know that he was also a coach at Boston University, a Division One hockey power. After the game ended, Jack called me aside and asked me what my plans were and I told him I was going to Merrimack. He said, 'We have a kid from Canada who's decided not to come to BU. Would you like his scholarship?'

"Well, of course I said yes, and I went in the next day and signed a $3,500 full scholarship with Boston University. The rest is history. The reason that's my Invincible Moment is that if I had phoned it in for that meaningless August hockey game, Jack Parker would have never given me a second look. I wouldn't have gone to BU and I probably would never have made the Olympic team. My life would have been very different.

"Instead, I've led a blessed life. I've had movies made about my team. I was part of what was voted the greatest sports moment in U.S. history. I scored the winning goal against the Soviet Union. I've had the honor of hearing my national anthem played from the podium. But the greatest honor was marching in the opening ceremonies at Lake Placid. If I hadn't played hard in that summer game, none of that would have happened.

"Everybody gets opportunities. It's what you do with them that matters. Any opportunity is worth exactly what you make of it."

## HOW TO CELEBRATE

Want to know the quickest way to get your butt handed to you in professional sports? Show up the guys on the other team. In the NFL, it used to be that a receiver who did an elaborate touchdown celebration on the field would get his head handed to him by the other team's defensive players at the first opportunity. That's why the league passed rules to penalize excessive celebrating (and why some say that NFL stands for "No Fun League").

In baseball, if you stand and watch one of your own home runs for too long, you're certain to get drilled in the ribs with a fastball the next time you come to the plate.

Celebrating a little is fine, but when you're rubbing the other team's nose in it you're asking for a fight.

The idea in celebrating your small wins is to use them to lift other people up along with yourself. Use your experience as an example of what other people you know can achieve. Spread your positive energy to friends or colleagues so they feel a morale boost, too. Or just take some work pals out and spring for dinner. The idea is to elevate other people so they see that there's reason to hope. In changing, challenging times like these, hope is hard to come by. Everybody's trying to find some. If you can be a vendor of it for just a few people, you're doing something really important.

Other than that, there really are no rules to celebrating your victories. Do something that makes you feel good. Some people treat themselves to a workout. Others take themselves out for an expensive dinner. Still others call in sick for the first time all year and reward themselves with a mental health day. Do whatever turns you on, provided it doesn't set back your bigger goal. If you're celebrating one year sober, I wouldn't suggest going on an all-night bender. That's all I'm saying.

## WHY TO CELEBRATE

**JANET:** When things are changing fast and you're not sure what the future holds, it's more important than ever to cheer the little wins. It reinforces that you can feel good about yourself, and that can help you get past negative feelings. We all need that kind of reinforcement, because nobody's so strong that they can go months or years without some sort of congratulations.

Another reason that smelling the roses is a very positive thing is that it focuses you on the small steps you've already taken toward your goal. If things aren't good and you look at the big picture, you might be overwhelmed. Giving yourself credit for something you've done well reminds you that even if you seem to be standing still, you're not. That can keep your eyes on the steps in front of you.

This is also a great tonic for anxiety. It reassures you that things are not as bad as you feared. They rarely are. Anxiety can tear you apart with the fear of what might happen but probably won't. Vince suffered from tremendous anxiety for years until he began to think he was mentally ill. That's one of the reasons he started getting his masters in counseling—to understand his own anxiety.

When times are tough or things are changing faster than you're comfortable with, you can start fearing the unknown that you can't control. That's anxiety. That's when you start celebrating making it from day to day. Instead of asking, "What's the worst thing that could happen?" you flip it on its head and ask, "What's the best thing that could happen?" Then you think about the good things that have already happened and realize that everything might just turn out all right.

It's also really smart to have someone around who reminds you to be good to yourself and who's strong when you're weak. Just knowing you're not the only one working your way and doing your best in changing times can make all the difference.

## HAVE THE LAST LAUGH

**VINCE:** Laugh at yourself. That's what Denny Franks and I are doing in that picture. We're laughing at the amazing place we found ourselves in: a couple of stiffs playing for the honest-to-God Philadelphia Eagles. How can you not laugh at something outrageous and fantastic?

If you're trying your best with honesty and courage, then you are doing what you can to take control and change your life. That it hasn't happened yet doesn't mean it won't. You've got to laugh. Stop taking yourself so seriously. Let yourself feel good about what you've done and how far you've come. That's really what this chapter is about: being good to yourself, being charitable and compassionate to yourself. Start there and you'll be amazed at how good you feel.

*Denny Franks and me celebrating after a big play to seal the deal. The "Last Laugh" hangs in the Pro Football Hall of Fame in Canton, Ohio.*

## END ZONE

**Things to think about & do after finishing this chapter**

■ Make a list of all the things you've done in the last week that you could celebrate.

_____

_____

_____

_____

_____

■ Write down the ways you can use your celebrations to lift up other people who need it.

_____

_____

_____

_____

_____

■ List the ways that your small wins have brought you even a tiny bit closer to your eventual goals.

_____

_____

_____

_____

_____

# CHAPTER SIXTEEN

# WHO'S ON YOUR TEAM?

*"A real friend is one who walks in when the rest of the world walks out."*

— Walter Winchell

For some guys, the physical part of life is easy. That's the way it was for me. I've always been fast, fit, and healthy as a horse, even after colon cancer. Relationships with women…well, those were another matter. In my younger days, I always seemed to have a way of hooking up with the wrong lady for the wrong reasons, pissing her off, and winding up alone.

I've told you about the way my first wife left me with a devastating note that left my confidence shattered. I had another seven-year marriage that ended poorly and after that I was drifting. I got to know myself a little better through analysis and learned about the things I did that set women off. But I didn't realize how screwed up I really was—or how much time I was spending feeling sorry for myself—until I met Janet in 1992.

I had been out of football for 13 years at that point. I had a great job as fitness director for U.S. Healthcare, the giant HMO. It was my job to train their top executives and keep them in the best health and fitness they could be in so they could perform better on the job. That's a pretty enlightened attitude for any employer. I loved the work, but I didn't love the fact that I seemed to be sinking as a person. I was dabbling in the mortgage business, but I was only marginally successful at that. I was down after my divorce, with a lot of self-doubt. I was deep in debt. My credit rating sucked. I wasn't sure what I wanted to do with the rest of my life. Outwardly, I was a smiling Philadelphia legend, the local boy made good who was always getting free beers from Eagles fans. Inwardly, I felt lost and confused. I was a wreck.

I first met Janet Cantwell in 1976 at the home of Jack Kelly, a four-time Olympic medal winner in the scull. Janet was a member of the USA World Gymnastics team at that time and had already coached and taught gymnastics all over the world, so she wasn't impressed by me. Nothing clicked between us, so we went our separate ways.

Our paths crossed again in 1992 when we were both serving on the board of a nonprofit organization that provided after-school activities for children. At that time in my life, I was desperately unhappy. Janet was working as a successful real estate agent, but I was deeper in debt than ever. I had this veneer that let me walk into a room and take it over, but it was all a lie. I had collection guys calling me saying, "You thought you were a big shot football player, but now you're a loser." I would completely blow my stack at these scumbags, partially because it felt like they might be right. I'd been the toast of the town, but what was I now? A lost, broke ex-athlete? Was that all I was? Doomed to be another statistic?

To her credit, Janet saw right through my veneer. She's the same kind of person: strong, with a powerful personality and zero tolerance for bullshit, but fragile underneath. She was the first woman to come into my life and say, "You're a pretty frustrated guy." We talked for a while and she finally said, "What can I do to help you out?"

I said jokingly, "Get me out of debt." Well, would you believe that this woman said let's work on it's together, we did, and eventually I was debt free. Right then and there I knew I wasn't dealing with an ordinary person. This was a lady who saw the problem, tackled it head-on and together we fixed it ... as a team. We started dating, and right away I discovered something really important about Janet. A lot of my past relationships had been ruined because the woman would be jealous of all the attention I would receive when we went out in Philly. I was still a big local celebrity. But Janet was never threatened by it. She was too confident in herself, and she knew what was behind my big grin and firm handshake.

After a few months, we went to the O Bar in Palm Beach, Florida, and decided to have what I called our "come to Jesus" meeting. I told her that I was going to lay all cards on the table about my past, former marriages, money and so on. She would get a full picture of what was true and untrue about me. She said the same thing. We laid our souls bare and it was okay. We were really, truly good with each other as we were. I had a soul mate. The fear I had always harbored about exposing myself to someone was gone.

## A ONE-MAN TEAM

**JANET:** My personal team came together very differently. I was getting ready to drive to Los Angeles to work press operations for the 1984 Olympic gymnastics. Right before I left, I had to have my car inspected. It didn't pass, and the dealer wanted $400 to repair it. I refused, since my car was only six months old. Just then I saw an elegant older gentleman drive up in this beautiful white Supra, and I said to him, "Don't get your car worked on here, they rip you off!"

The gentleman turned out to be one of the owners of the dealership, Central City Toyota. His name was Gil, and we spent a lot of time talking. He was 77, had just lost his wife to cancer, and he was lonely. I told him that I was the head gymnastics coach at Penn, and it turned out that he was a former gymnast. I told him I wanted his dealership to sponsor my team, and he said he would help me. He got my car done in two days and I was off to California.

When I returned home, Gil became my team's sponsor and my mentor. It gave him a purpose after his wife died, and it helped a young college coach find her way. Gilly got me to try golf, which I now love to play with Vince and our children. I will always be indebted to my dear friend, Gil Schulman, because he gave me the skills and confidence to be the successful businesswoman that I am today.

This was all because I was nice to him on a street corner. Because of a simple act of kindness to a gentle elderly man, Gil became my one-man support team, mentor, advisor and advocate and encouraged me to try something new. He taught me to be the negotiator I am today.

## YOUR PEOPLE ARE YOUR FOUNDATION

**VINCE:** As you're preparing yourself to leverage your potential during changing times, one of the most important edges you can give yourself is to surround yourself with good people who believe in and support you no matter what.

With Janet, I know that she's behind anything I throw myself into. She's so strong intellectually and physically, that she can be intimidating to some people. We have a great relationship. We both come from families that, like many others, had issues. We've both been coaches and teachers and reached the highest level of a sport after being told that we could never get there. We're the only spouses to have been inducted into the Pennsylvania Sports Hall of Fame.

Part of what makes our relationship work for me is that Janet has no fear about calling me out. When I found out about my colon cancer in 2001, I was feeling sorry for myself. Janet got in my face and said,

"You're supposed to be this courageous, tough guy. You're just a blubbering idiot. Be who you say you are." That snapped me to attention right away!

If you're going to be successful in life, you have to surround yourself with people who grow with you. Most couples divorce because they don't grow as a team. When you come home you need someone who believes in you and fills you up. In hard times like a recession, people carry around a lot of self-doubt; they may have lost their jobs or be making a salary that's half of what they used to make. When things like that happen, you need a good foundation of people—spouse, friends, family members—to help you deal with the stress and find the confidence to keep going.

When you grow together and something happens in your life, you meet it together. This even applies to events that anyone would see as positive. When the movie *Invincible* came out, we got slammed with an avalanche of attention. There was a backlash among some people who

*It's all about teamwork as me and 3 other bomb squadders blow up a Redskins return man.*

were jealous that I had a Hollywood movie made about me, and my children have felt some of this as well. The truth is, some people will resent you because of your strength and success. That's why you've got to have a team of people behind you who love and support you no matter what.

Your people are your teammates in life. I would have been nothing without all the incredible people who helped me train to make the Eagles, without pros like Denny Franks and Harold Carmichael who passed along invaluable tips, without my teammates who made it possible for me to have a job at all, and without the family and friends who gave me a reason to play every Sunday. When you're preparing for life's changes, build a strong team that will be there for you in the bad times, not just the good.

## FINDING THE RIGHT PEOPLE

Sometimes, finding the right people is a matter of being at the right place at the right time. But more often, you'll find the people you want on your team all around you already. I know that my journey to the NFL wouldn't have been possible without the help of old friends from my neighborhood, from my high school, my college and my recreational football league. So many people helped me that I've lost count. We had mutual respect—I respected their passion and they respected how I played the game.

### JANET'S WORDS FOR WOMEN

*Your team can change at any time, and people can come together in ways that you never expect. The team that helped bring this book about came together because we had an opportunity and took it. Women are especially good at bringing people together; leverage that. If people believe in your idea, they will come together around it.*

Basically, if you're looking for folks who will stick with you through thick and thin, you should be looking for character above everything else. To me, character is all about authenticity—being who you say you are, owning up to your flaws and not being ashamed of them, and always bringing your best to the situation, even if you end up falling on your ass. It means being 100% real and 100% honest about what you want, what you can do and what you care about. That's why so many of the people on my team to this day are guys I've known for years. We get each other. Every one of us knows when one of the group is getting a big ego or not being honest about something. We don't let each other get away with anything.

The right people are also the ones who inspire you because of how they live their lives. None of us is perfect; we all fall short in some way. The brilliant musician might be a disaster as a father. The million-

## INVINCIBLE MOMENT

*Betty Thesky, host of the popular podcast "Betty in the Sky with a Suitcase," has been a flight attendant for nearly a quarter of a century. The following is from her book of the same name:*

*"I took a trip with a friend to Morocco. We had already enjoyed some amazing adventures during the first week of our journey and were about to board a train from Fez to Meknes. It is an hour-long train ride and we decided to splurge and purchase first class tickets. We had to share the first class cabin with a Frenchman and his wife…My friend and I had an idea which hotel we would stay in Meknes and knew the next train stop after that was Casablanca, four hours later. We got our duffel bags ready before the train pulled into the station, knowing that the trains make quick stops and passengers need to be ready to exit in a hurry. The train came to a stop but there was a Moroccan*

woman in front of me. The French man started yelling at me, 'Get off the train, get off the train!'

"I put my foot out and jumped. I didn't roll like in the movies. My landing was far less glorious. I went splat with arms and legs akimbo and duffel bag and backpack flying every which way. Time was moving slowly as I noticed parts from my broken camera on the pavement and my blood splattered on the ground. Then I turned to look at train to see it picking up speed, with my friend leaning out of the open door, mouth agape at my predicament, and the French man's eyes wide. They hadn't gotten off the train!

"I had just lost my friend in a foreign country where I didn't speak the language. What would I do now? I gathered myself up, got to a bench, took inventory of my (mostly minor) injuries, and started bandaging my wounds. At this point two train station employees came out and stood in front of me. They spoke French and I gathered they were saying, 'Why did you jump off the train?' I was trying to explain…when I saw my friend and the French man running toward me! "Are you okay?" she asked as we hugged. What we didn't know was that there were two stops in Meknes!

"What I didn't realize at the time was that 30 minutes at the train stop, alone, hurt, confused, and unable to communicate, had a profound effect on me. I realized I could be alone and in trouble and I could figure what to do on my own. Three months after that, I took my first international trip by myself. Since then I have not only learned that I can travel alone, but that I love it! Traveling alone has empowered me to take many other bold steps in my life. I got my first book published and have been interviewed by NPR and the BBC. Who knew that jumping off a train would bring about such profound changes?"

aire entrepreneur could be an obese heart attack waiting to happen. Every one of us needs people who excel at the areas of life where we don't do so well. Why? Because we can look at them and say, "I want to be like you." With their help, maybe we can train for and finish that 10K race or get up and speak in front of 10,000 people, something that's easy for me but downright terrifying for some folks.

My final criterion for a member of my team is simple: be positive. Negative people suck the energy right out of a room. You know what I mean? Everybody is pumped up about some idea or other and then someone comes along and sticks a needle in the balloon. He's trying to look wise or experienced or something, but what he really does is sabotage everybody's self-belief. Being negative does not mean you're wise or see things more clearly than the rest of us, or that you never gave up hope. It means you're afraid to stick your neck out and risk failing, even though that also means you have zero chance of succeeding.

Positive thinking and a positive attitude lend confidence. Being positive is a way of saying that you trust someone to get the job done, even if the odds say they can't. Doesn't everybody deserve that opportunity? I don't want anyone on my team who's not positive and encouraging about what I can do.

By the way, there is a difference between being positive and being a Pollyanna, and being negative and being a realist. You want realists on your team; if you're tone-deaf, you don't need butt-kissers telling you to quit your job and move to Nashville to pursue your singing career. But don't just tell me why something isn't a good risk—offer a solution. Come up with an alternative. Keep me grounded but give me options. That's being a great teammate.

## GET RID OF THE WRONG PEOPLE

Just as important as choosing the right people is getting rid of the wrong ones. If you're not around people who believe in you, get away from them. People will judge you by who you associate with, so if you want to be seen as a hard-driving professional but you still hang out with the same slackers who were your dorm buddies in college, you might want to start rethinking that association.

I know from experience that the wrong people will fill you with negative talk, try to sabotage you, and cheer when things go wrong for you. I've seen it. Someone excels at her job and her colleagues accuse her of making them look bad. One player out-hustles the rest of the guys and gets hazed in the locker room because he's "showing them up." There are plenty of classic "bad teammates" to choose from, and you might recognize some of them in your own life:

- The party boy who's rude, crude and makes you look bad in front of others.

- The downer who's always finding the reasons something will fail.

- The ball dropper who never seems to hold up his end of the bargain.

- The whiner who complains constantly.

- The know-it-all who never listens to anyone else.

- The moralizer who turns around and cheats, steals and lies.

You can probably name a few others, but you get the idea. Simply, good people are going to be happy for you when you do well, and the better you do, the more excited and happy they will be. Your success doesn't diminish them. If you have people in your life who seem to be threatened or embarrassed by your achievements, it's time to cut them from your team.

How? Simple. Stop returning their calls. Quit replying to their emails. Limit your contact. Quit sharing important details of your life with them. You might feel like a heel at first, but be firm and you'll get over it. This isn't high school; you don't need a BFF. You need people who you can go to war with, knowing they've got your back. If anybody in your circle doesn't meet that standard, cut him or her loose without guilt.

## HOW TO BUILD YOUR TEAM

When Dick Vermeil set about trying to rebuild a terrible Philadelphia Eagles team in 1976, he did some very smart things. First, he held open tryouts and invited about 120 people to camp, about 40 more than normal. Then he made his training camp one of the most brutal affairs ever seen on a football field, so that he would be able to weed out the guys who really wanted to be there from the guys who "sort of" wanted to play ball. It was grim. During three-hour practice sessions in full pads, guys were passing out and vomiting in the heat. That's why Vermeil brought so many players to camp; the drill lines were the only time that anybody could catch his breath, so he wanted the lines to be extra long. Smart, smart strategies, and they paid off. By the time the team broke camp, Coach knew that everybody on the team wanted to be there more than anything, including yours truly.

> ### INVINCIBLE WISDOM
>
> *"A positive attitude may not solve all your problems, but it will annoy enough people to make it worth the effort."*
>
> — Herm Albright, Reader's Digest, June 1995

Build your own team the same way:

- **Look for certain roles.** A football team has offensive players, defensive players and special teams. It has blockers, return guys, and other specialists. When you're building your team, it's helpful to have people in your life who can give you the various things you need. You might want an organizer who can get things done and communicate with everybody. You might want a cheerleader who thinks and talks positive no matter what. You might want a truth teller who can be counted on to keep it real and quickly pull you out of any delusions you might have. You might love to have a coach or motivator who kicks your butt. Think of the roles you want on your team, and find players who can perform them.

- **Demand the best.** I'm not suggesting that you come up with tests and trials to put your friends and family through. That would be pretty cold and heartless. What I'm suggesting is that you hold the people in your life to a high standard, starting now. Ask yourself what you're willing to tolerate and why. What are you not willing to tolerate, and why not? Start looking critically at the people in your life, the choices they make and their motivations. You'll start identifying the ones who are real winners with courage and character, and the ones who just sort of muddle through. Spend more of your time with the winners.

- **Have a game plan.** When you start to see the people who really help you elevate your game, talk to them. Tell them about your goals, share your admiration for them, and ask them for their help. They'll be flattered, believe me. You're basically doing what a head coach does: sharing your game plan and getting your players to buy into it. That's how winning happens.

Two more tips before I wrap up this chapter. First, be prepared to be a leader on someone else's team, too. This isn't just about you; we're all in this life together. Make sure you're a great teammate and you'll find great teammates. Second, every winning team begins with your spouse or partner. Make sure you commit to someone who makes you better, supports you no matter what, and complements your strengths. That's what I've found. I hope you're as fortunate.

## END ZONE

**Things to think about & do after finishing this chapter**

■ Write out the various roles you'd like to fill on your team.

_____

_____

_____

_____

_____

_____

■ List the people—friends, family, colleagues—who you consider to be part of your current team.

_____

_____

_____

_____

_____

_____

_____

■ Match some of them to roles that they're suited to fill.

_____

_____

_____

_____

_____

## END ZONE

■ Take the rest and look at them with a critical eye. Are there people who bring you down, talk negatively or make you look bad? Consider ways to reduce your contact with them or get them out of your life.

_____

_____

_____

_____

_____

■ Write down some of the goals you'd like your teammates to help you accomplish and how you'll get there.

_____

_____

_____

_____

_____

_____

_____

_____

_____

_____

# CHAPTER SEVENTEEN

# STAY OUT
## OF THE
# BUCKET OF CRABS

*"An injured friend is the bitterest of foes."*

— Thomas Jefferson

When I do speaking engagements for companies like Rite-Aid, one of the most popular parts of my speech is usually where I talk about what I call the "bucket of crabs." Now, if you're from a landlocked area or the closest you come to live seafood is Long John Silver's, I'll explain.

When you fill a bucket with crabs, the first few you put in there will try to crawl out. That's a natural survival instinct. But when you put more and more crabs in, for some reason they will stop trying to get out. They mostly give up and sit there, waiting to be cooked. If a crab gets ambitious and decides that he really wants out—maybe he's got the Tivo set to record an episode of *Desperate Housewives* or something—the other crabs will actually try to pull him back into the bucket. If you try to take the top crab out, the others will hold on and try to keep you from freeing the little bugger!

Another good example comes from the first *Toy Story* movie. Remember when Woody and Buzz Lightyear were at the pizza place and wound up inside that game where you grab a toy with the mechanical claw? Sid, the sadistic neighbor kid, got Buzz in the claw and was reeling him in, all set for future torture. Woody tried to free Buzz, but then those alien dolls grabbed him and pulled him back down into the crowd. Sid got Buzz and nearly blew him to smithereens.

### JANET'S WORDS FOR WOMEN

*Women get emotionally attached to things, while men can engage and stay on the surface more easily. That's why we get hurt more easily when people lash out at us for our successes or failures. Plus, women are more likely to go after you in a subtle way, while men are direct. You have to have a thicker skin in this world as a woman than as a man. You can't let betrayal or envy get to you.*

## PEOPLE ARE THE CRABS

Well, some people in your life will be just like the crabs in that bucket or the aliens in that game. They don't want you to be successful because it makes them feel bad about themselves. Maybe they never achieved the things you have. Maybe they're embarrassed that they

175

*"It stirs up envy, fame does. People feel fame gives them some kind of privilege to walk up to you and say anything to you and it won't hurt your feelings, like it's happening to your clothing."*

— *Marilyn Monroe*

didn't have the courage to go for their dreams like you did. Maybe they're just small in spirit. Whatever the reason, I can practically guarantee you that no matter how nice a person you are, no matter how generous you are with your money and time, there will always be people who want to tear you down or tell you that you can't do something. They are your crabs.

Back in the chapter on building your team, I talked a little bit about identifying such people and getting them out of your life, but it's such an important subject—and I'm painfully familiar with it from personal experience—that I thought it deserved a chapter all its own.

My experiences with the crabs left me emotionally bruised at first. I honestly couldn't understand how anybody from my hometown of Philadelphia could bear me any ill will for making the Eagles. Here I was, a nobody from the projects, a blue-collar Italian kid like Rocky Balboa, and I was representing every other guy who'd ever had a dream about playing pro football. I made it clear that I was taking bone-rattling hits and playing my heart out for my fellow nose bleeders in the cheap seats, the people I loved. I assumed that everybody felt the love. But I was wrong.

In the movie, there's a character named Johnny who says to me, "You're not one of us." Johnny is a combination of several people I had known for years who, as soon as I got a little bit of fame, turned on me. I guess they were bitter, because if you're insecure about all the things you haven't been able to do in your own life, seeing somebody else's success just magnifies your failures. The only way to deal with that for most people is to lash out in anger.

It's a very American thing to build up our heroes and then immediately start tearing them down. Look at Lance Armstrong. The guy had an incredible career after surviving what was supposed to be fatal testicular cancer, but as soon as he hangs up his bike his former friends are testifying before grand juries about his alleged doping. As I write this, one of the most inspiring athletes in American history is facing a possible federal indictment. As soon as there was a sign of weakness, the wolves started ripping at him.

## THE GREEN-EYED MONSTER

**JANET:** I think that no matter how hard you try, there will always be people who want to pull you back down to their level. Misery definitely loves company.

I've had a wonderful life. I don't know if it's because I almost died at nine years old, but I'm grateful. I like helping people be the best they can be. But success can make other people feel inadequate. They say they chose not to go after some dream or other, but I say they're full of it. They didn't want to risk failing, or they didn't know where to start. Some insist they didn't have the energy. Well, I believe that every day you get an opportunity, even if you don't know it. Always say yes to it, because you don't know if it will come around again.

**VINCE:** Those kinds of jealousies came up for me when *Invincible* came out in 2006. But there's usually nothing you can do to stop some people from becoming crabs in your life. The problem is them, not you. Here's what to look out for:

- People who start to say things designed to undermine your confidence. They're usually afraid that your success will remind them of their own insecurities.

- Requests to not let your star shine so brightly. It always amazes me when I hear about people in a workplace or school asking a high achiever to stop being quite so good in order to make everyone else look less bad.

- Backstabbing. If you hear through the grapevine that someone has been spreading rumors about you, you can bet it's someone who wants to see you fail.

What really hurts is when the people trying to pull you back into the bucket are friends you thought you could trust. That's why, when I became famous, the bitterness of some of the guys from my old stomping grounds was so hard to take. All I wanted was to make them feel good and express my love and respect, but they couldn't get past their own feelings of inadequacy. Watch for the warning signs and you can protect yourself.

## BEWARE THE POSSE

Crabs mostly hurt you in two ways: trashing your confidence or making you feel guilty for making them look bad, getting a big ego and leaving them behind (which is the way they see it). But there's another way they can injure you that can actually be a lot more damaging, and that's by becoming your posse.

Ever watch the TV show *Entourage*? If your buddies ever become the kind of hangers-on who think you're their gravy train, you're in trouble. Even if you're not a celebrity, this sort of thing can happen. Let's say you run a small business and send some of your sales staff to a conference. While there they get drunk and say stupid things to some of your key customers. You're not there, but they are representing you, so it's your image and brand that get beaten up.

You've probably seen athletes and celebrities like this. They roll with a big posse of buddies who don't really seem to do anything but bask in their reflected celebrity. With other people, as soon as they begin experiencing some success their posse accused them of being egotistical sellouts. When boxing champion Oscar de la Hoya started winning titles and becoming a star, some people in his native East Los Angeles said that he was forgetting his roots. Yet there's nobody humbler or more proud of his background than Oscar.

## DEFYING THE CRABS

Most importantly, don't listen. The crabs in your life are negative people who look at the glass as half-empty. They count on you being tender hearted enough to feel sorry for them. Don't. The only thing that will make them happy is seeing you fail, and that's the sort of

# INVINCIBLE MOMENT

*Janet's sister Barbara Cantwell-Wheeler shares her own Invincible Moment:*

"My Invincible Moment occurred when my big sister Janet invited me to team up with her at the University of Pennsylvania. Although Janet was still only in the early stages of building a gymnastics team there, she convinced me to give up my full athletic scholarship to Oklahoma State University and transfer to Penn so that she could coach me and I could help her build her new program. I saw it as a unique opportunity to be my best in a supportive environment, and knew I had to make it work. The Ivy League does not offer athletic scholarships, so transferring to Penn was a great financial hardship because I gave up a full scholarship at OSU. I sacrificed a lot but it was worth it. Luckily I was able to enroll as a sophomore transfer student into the Wharton school.

"It wasn't always easy training with my sister as my coach: she knew me well and seemed to work me harder and expect more from me than from anyone else. I didn't always give her the respect that she deserved, but in the end it was a very successful partnership. We were the first and only gymnast and coach sisters to represent Penn in our hometown of Philadelphia.

"Although I was never able to achieve my lifelong dream of becoming an Olympic gymnast, with the encouragement, help and mentoring of my sister Janet, I was able to adjust my goals and still be happy with the outcome. I did get my BS in economics from the Wharton School, and with Janet's coaching I was the first Penn gymnast to qualify and compete at the collegiate nationals. I was the three-time winner of the Ivy League all-around gymnastics championships, and received many awards including the Fathers' Trophy and the Harnwell Award. In 2001 I was inducted into the University of Pennsylvania Athletic Hall of Fame."

*"A competent and self-confident person is incapable of jealousy in anything. Jealousy is invariably a symptom of neurotic insecurity."*

— *Robert A. Heinlein*

person who doesn't deserve to be in your life. Dump them, sever ties, change your number, whatever you have to do. Just as important, stick to your guns. Don't change a thing about what you do or how you do it. If you're having success, there will be a lot more people who will be genuinely thrilled for you. That's really important to remember. We tend to lend more weight to the negative. If we write a paper at work and pass it around to 20 people, and 19 say it's brilliant but one says it's terrible, who do we listen to? The critic. That's human nature, but you can train yourself not to listen. Instead, remember that for every person who's a crab trying to drag you back into the bucket, there are probably 20 or 50 or 100 people who are applauding and bragging about you to their friends.

One other critical piece of advice that's unique to the modern age: ignore critics on the Internet. I'm always shocked at the degree of rage and filth and bile I see on online comment boards, blogs and discussion forums, and that comes from people being able to say things anonymously. Believe me, if some of those "expert critics" had to walk up to me or another ex-player and fire off the same insults to our faces, they'd think twice. Being invisible makes bloggers feel brave and untouchable. If someone unleashes a stream of venom at you on the Internet, remember that it's probably someone who's not one tenth of what you are. Feel sorry for them and move on. I used to lose sleep over it ... not any more!

Last word: be careful not to dismiss all criticism as sour grapes. Just because someone lays into you or your work doesn't mean he's ignorant or jealous. Consider the source. If it's someone whose opinion or knowledge you respect, take it more seriously. It would be foolish to reject feedback that might help you become better at what you do.

## END ZONE

Things to think about & do after finishing this chapter

■ Write the names of the people who you know will support you no matter what. That's your A team.

_____

_____

_____

_____

■ Write the names of the people who will support you when times are good, but not so much when things get tight. That's your B team.

_____

_____

_____

_____

■ Write the names of anyone you know who you think might envy you or try to undermine you when things go well. Those are the people you cut from your roster if they get ugly.

_____

_____

_____

_____

■ List the things you do exceptionally well, or your greatest current personal successes. This will be your reminder of what to keep doing should bitter personal criticism come your way.

_____

_____

_____

_____

# CHAPTER EIGHTEEN

# FAIL FORWARD

*"There are no failures, just experiences and your reactions to them."*

— Tom Krause

One of the reasons I was successful in my effort to make the Eagles was that I had nothing to lose. I didn't fear failure. I didn't want to fail, because becoming a pro football player had always been my dream, but if I got cut, the world wasn't going to end. I would go back to teaching, get my counseling degree and life would go on. That lack of fear freed me to give it everything I had. I was determined that if Coach Vermeil did give me the heave-ho (and the odds were definitely stacked against me), it would be because I was too old, there were too many guys in camp more talented than me, or just the politics of roster decisions. It wouldn't be because I hadn't put out enough effort.

The way I've always seen it, you never fail when you give everything you have to achieve something, because even if you don't reach your goal, you grow. You learn things about yourself, including what your limits are. You gain the respect of others, because everyone appreciates somebody who spends blood, sweat, muscle, bone and time to try to make something good happen, even if it doesn't work out. Let me tell you this from a pro athlete's standpoint: when I was playing, we didn't give a damn about "hustle mistakes." When a player went all-out to make a tackle, catch a pass or block a punt, even if he failed, we had his back in the locker room. Effort earns respect even in failure. What nobody would ever tolerate was a slacker, somebody showboating and not trying. If you didn't give 120% on the field, even if you got lucky and caught the pass, we'd eat you alive later on.

## NATURE'S GREATEST CLASSROOM

Nothing teaches better than failure. Think about it: when you do something right, are you interesting in reflecting and learning? No! You're busy pounding your chest, high-fiving everybody and planning the perfect time to ask for that raise. It's only when we drop the ball that we get introspective and start asking the questions that wind up making us wiser and better. Mental anguish is a great motivator of self-improvement. Did you blow it because you didn't take care of the fundamentals? Were you not prepared? Did you get nervous because you're human? Did you drop the ball because the lights were in your eyes or the crowd distracted you? Most important, how can you

*"I didn't fail ten thousand times. I successfully eliminated, ten thousand times, materials and combinations which wouldn't work."*

— *Thomas Edison on inventing the light bulb*

improve so that the next time, you don't fail?

That's how improvement happens. That's why athletes in every sport go over film or tape of their performance after every game. We all make mistakes, but in those mistakes lie the seeds of success. The key is to not be so afraid of failure that you resolve never to try again. No one likes a quitter. Quitting is the one sure way to guarantee that you'll never achieve what you want in life.

How many people have you known who said, "Well, I wanted to be such-and-such when I was in school, but I studied business instead so I could get a job." That's B.S. The truth is, most of those people knew what they were passionate about but feared the risk of going after it. No, it's not easy to become a pro football player, a singer or an astronaut; if it was, everybody would do it! But imagine looking back for the rest of your life and feeling like you cheated yourself out of the life you could have had because you chickened out. We don't regret the things we attempt, but the things we don't attempt. Regret is a terrible burden and I pity anyone who carries it. That's one of the main reasons I tried out for the Eagles: I wanted to be able to look back and know that I'd gone for it.

**JANET:** I was always full of energy, muscle, and determination. I had trouble sitting still in a classroom long enough for anyone to realize that I was smart until much later in life. I was a hard worker, with a strong personality. I stood out in my family, not just because I was the firstborn, but because I was bold, loud and full of personality and determination. I never gave up. I was the underdog that you rooted for and wanted to succeed because the odds seemed stacked against me. I had to work hard for everything, and I reveled in the work.

I wanted to win, and I didn't care about failure. I wanted to be something special and gymnastics was my platform. It was my garden, my art. I loved the sweat and the exertion. It was all joy for me. I wasn't a good student like my sisters were, so sports were where I excelled. I didn't worry about failure, because nobody but me ever expected me to be anything. I took education, knowledge and opportunity from everywhere I could, but I never compromised who I was.

## FAILURE AND SELF-ESTEEM

One of the greatest problems with our society is that we're teaching our children to fear failure. We do it with the best of intentions, because we want our kids to be happy and not have the same hardships that we experienced. But instead, we're teaching them that if they can't be perfect at something right away, they shouldn't even bother with it! We're training them to avoid risks, and if they do take a risk and fall on their asses, we're hovering over them ready to pick them up and make sure they don't experience any negative consequences.

Well, I don't think I have to tell you that if you have kids, the best way to ensure that they grow up to be helpless, entitled adults is to bail them out every time they screw up. Kids make mistakes; mine certainly have. That's how they learn! So your kid doesn't study for a test and gets an F. You let them fail. Consequences are fantastic teachers. The best thing we can do when our kids, employees or players fail is allow them to do it, help them see what caused the failure, suggest steps they can take to fix the problem, then step back and give them the chance to prove themselves. Back in the day they called it P.E.T. - Parent Effectiveness Training. That's how people improve over time. They get humbled, step back, collect themselves, analyze the situation and find ways to get it done.

We try to spare our kids from failure as a way to bolster their self-esteem, but that's misguided. Self-esteem doesn't come from mommy and daddy making sure that Junior gets all As in school and gets accepted to Harvard because of family connections. Self-esteem grows when people overcome obstacles and failures to achieve their goals. That's it. When kids fall down, dust themselves off, try a new strategy to solve a problem, put out maximum effort, and succeed, they feel incredible pride and a sense of accomplishment. That's what creates self-esteem. When we don't allow our kids to fail, we're denying them the chance to really grow.

JANET: That's why sports is so great. It teaches you how to win, but even more important is that it teaches you how to lose. You can lose in a controlled environment with coaches who (if they're good) won't let you run away from the reasons why you lost. When I was a gymnastics coach at Penn, hundreds of companies wanted to employ my former athletes because they were self-directed and knew how to take criticism and turn it into a positive. That's character.

We could use more of it. Vince does team building workshops for corporations and in most cases, when you watch the team in action, 5% of the people do 90% of the work. The rest are too afraid of failing to stick their necks out and risk not being perfect. Who needs perfect? You just have to make the effort and give it your best! I'll bet you if you asked those people sitting on their hands if their parents shielded them from failure when they were kids, most would say yes.

## INVINCIBLE MOMENT

*Marine Corps veteran Capt. Bryce McDonald honors us with his recollection of his own Invincible Moment:*

*"The last memory I have is of calling in a suspicious vehicle to be searched. Then...BOOM. I wake upside down. My body is in shock. I pray. My door swings open. First Sergeant Huckobey is standing over me. He cracks a joke. We spend what seems to be five minutes trying to pry my body out of the Humvee. He carries a limp 265 lbs. out of the kill zone. The man is a hero. He sets security and calls for the quick reaction force, all with a cool smile on his face. Thank you, First Sergeant.*

*"The doc runs out of morphine, then hands me an 800mg Motrin. We laugh. I love Marines. The helicopter lands. We are loaded and off to the closest base. I feel like I am letting my Marines down by leaving.*

"My next memory is of a female Air Force nurse sternly telling me to gain composure while I was lying on the stainless steel table in the triage center at an unknown base in Iraq. I am lying next to one of my Marines who is screaming. I am trying to let him know I am next to him. A SEAL corpsman injects something into my IV...fade to black...

"I wake up a couple days later to a nurse informing me that my wife is on the phone. She tries to hide her concern. She had given birth to our daughter two weeks before. She has already been briefed by the doctor: he told her my leg is severely damaged and that I have a good chance of losing it. We are not concerned about the leg; people run marathons with fake ones. We mainly speak about our new daughter, Kayleigh Belle McDonald. After the phone call, I pray. Then more black, more surgery.

"I wake up, look over and see that the Army vs. Navy football game happens to be on. I used to play for Navy; we win. More comfort. I have no memory of the trip from Germany to the US.

"The first meeting with my wife and new daughter happens by chance in the hallway as I am coming out of another surgery. That moment is burned into my memory forever. Two angels, so beautiful. I pray and thank the Lord. Today, I have my leg, and a few months ago I ran my first mile. I have three healthy kids and a beautiful wife. I am in my last year as the operations officer for the Navy football team and then I am retiring from the Marine Corps.

"Alone I am weak. With my faith, family, Marines and friends, I am invincible."

# HERE COME DA JUDGE

**VINCE:** So why are so many people terrified of failure? I know that part of it is the immediate consequences. If you blow the presentation, maybe your company loses the client and you end up getting fired. But it goes deeper than that. People become paralyzed by failure even when the possible backlash is nothing more than feeling embarrassed. Why?

I think it's because we often view failure as an indictment of our character or ability. We take it personally and feel like the world is judging us and that we're not measuring up. If you do that, eventually you start anticipating rejection and failure, so you avoid risk altogether. You know how bad it felt the last time you dropped the ball; you felt like a complete loser. You don't want that feeling again, so it's safer to do what you know you're good at and not risk failing.

That's why, as Janet says, sports is wonderful. You know what happens when a wide receiver drops a wide-open touchdown pass in front of 60,000 screaming fans on national TV? He has to line up at scrimmage on the very next play and go for it again with the same intensity and abandon. If a relief pitcher in baseball blows a lead in the bottom of the ninth, he has to put that aside and run out to the mound the next night with the bases loaded and two out, ready to close the door. Sports makes you develop a short memory for failure. If you don't—if you go back on the field doubting or playing not to screw up—you're sunk. You won't bring your best and you won't perform at the level you're capable of.

### JANET'S WORDS FOR WOMEN

*You might have ten failures before your next big hit. Sometimes it's just about timing. In real estate, if you invest at the right time, you're a genius. If you invest at the wrong time, you're a loser. Women can take failure pretty hard, but try not to. It's not personal. It's not a verdict on your ability to be as good as a man. It's just what happens.*

Psychologist Martin Seligman developed a brilliant concept called learned helplessness that I think has everything to do with how we regard failure. Basically, he says that how we explain our failures determines how we respond to them and how we change our behavior. The pessimist sees failure as personal, pervasive and permanent—"It's all my fault, I can't do anything right, and it will never change." The optimist sees failure as impersonal,

incomplete and impermanent—"Lots of things went wrong, I'm still successful in other areas, and next time it will be better."

Seligman says that the positive or negative view of failure is a behavioral habit that people pick up over years. The key is that like any habit, you can choose to change it! It's not hard to see that having the pessimistic view of failure would be pretty crippling. If you believe that a hot man or woman saying "No" when you ask them out means you're hideous and will never be desirable to anyone ever again, you're going to lead a miserable, lonely life.

Part of being invincible through change is understanding that change will force you to take risks, and that in some of those risks, you'll fail. But that's not a judgment on you. It only means that you didn't succeed this time. The fact is, when you try and give it your best, you don't fail. It's only when you let fear control your decisions that you fail.

## WHAT FAILURE TEACHES US

What can we learn from failure? Here's a partial list of lessons courtesy of some hard personal experience:

> • **It's not the end of the world.** When you flop miserably, you expect the sky to fall. It doesn't, and you realize that life goes on. We can get so wrapped up in trying to succeed that we think if we don't, it invalidates all the other good things we've done. That's wrong. Your boss won't fire you (unless you really screwed up), your spouse will still speak to you, and the world will go on turning. You figure out that failure is not the end, but the beginning.

- **How to plan and prepare.** Nothing encourages us to plan, research, and get ready for an opportunity like botching the one that came before it. I guarantee you that if you have ever experienced a humiliating failure for lack of preparation, you have never made that mistake again. If anything, now you over-prepare. You anticipate what the other guy is doing. You have a Plan B. You have your charts, graphs and numbers. You don't ever want to get caught with your pants down again.

- **Humility.** We've all got egos, and when we pile up a few successes, it's very human to get cocky. We start to think we can just show and good things will happen. The trouble is, it doesn't work that way. The great baseball pioneer Branch Rickey said, "Luck is the residue of design." That means you plan, you work and then good things happen. A few failures strip you of that ego and remind you that nobody gets to the top by just showing up.

- **There's always something to take away.** Even when your plans fall totally flat, there's almost always something good that results. You get the business card of somebody who might make a perfect partner in the future. You learn new technology. You get in shape. You meet the person who becomes your spouse. That's why even when things go wrong, stay cool, professional and positive. You never know when the work you did with today's failure will become the foundation of tomorrow's success.

## FAIL BIG

He went bankrupt not once but twice. He lost four elections for the House of Representatives. He failed to be elected to the U.S. Senate twice. As a vice presidential candidate, he lost.

His name? Abraham Lincoln. Yeah, the guy regarded as the greatest U.S. president of all time.

Failure is a precursor to success. Ask any of the most successful people in this country—CEOs, bestselling authors, musicians, athletes, politicians, inventors—and they will all tell you that they failed many times before they finally broke through. Joe Torre had a record of 894-1003 as a baseball manager before he joined the New York Yankees in 1996; he led the Bronx

Bombers to six pennants and four World Series titles. Adventurer Steve Fossett tried five times to become the first person to fly around the world, nonstop and alone, in a balloon before he finally broke through on the sixth attempt in 2002.

Ernest Shackleton may be the most celebrated failure in history. When his ship Endurance was trapped in pack ice on an expedition to the Antarctic in 1914, he led his men from their doomed ship on an impossible journey in open boats to South Georgia Island, where they were finally rescued. Despite incredible hardships, freezing conditions and primitive equipment, Shackleton didn't lose a man. His failed expedition has become one of the great examples of courage and heroism.

The message here is simple: don't fear failure. If you're daring to try great things, you're going to fail. Fail big! Try bold things that will teach you, get you noticed, bring out the best in you and lead to your eventual success. You have a lot more to lose by not taking a risk than you do by running away from it and staying in your comfort zone.

**JANET:** Don't worry about the resentment of others who don't have the guts to hang it all out there. Most people want to be liked. They are pleasers. They would rather fit in with the mediocre people than stand out by being everything they can be. It's hard to be an outsider. But what are your options? To be on the outside looking in while other people do what you could have done?

I think it's much better to be on the inside looking out at the people who won't leave their safe places. When Vince and I were working on the movie *Invincible*, and I saw how some of his so-called friends treated him when he got famous, I asked him, "How did you stick with this when they were being so cruel to you? What got you to the next day?" He told me that what got him to the next day were the people in the stand, his students and the guys he played ball with. They were worth risking failure for.

## END ZONE

**Things to think about & do after finishing this chapter**

■ **Write down your three greatest failures and what you learned from them.**

_____

_____

_____

_____

_____

■ **Why did you fail in those instances? How have you changed things to prevent those mistakes?**

_____

_____

_____

_____

_____

_____

■ **List things you wish you had done in your life but didn't for fear of failing.**

_____

_____

_____

_____

_____

## END ZONE

■ **Describe a bold risk you could take that would change your life. What would be the potential damage from failure? What would be the potential payoff from success?**

_____

_____

_____

_____

_____

_____

_____

■ **What's stopping you?**

_____

_____

_____

_____

_____

_____

_____

_____

_____

_____

_____

# CHAPTER NINETEEN

# ANALYZE, ADAPT, ACHIEVE

*"Enjoying success requires the ability to adapt. Only by being open to change will you have a true opportunity to get the most from your talent."*

— Nolan Ryan

There was a scene in the movie *Invincible* that I've already referenced: the white knuckles scene. In the film, I was getting pounded in what was called the "nutcracker" drill. That actually wasn't true; I held my own, but the director needed to create some drama, which was okay by me. In the film, my pal Dennis Franks came up to me and told me that when I looked at the linemen opposite me, if their knuckles were white, that meant they were planning to charge the passer, which was true. They were leaning slightly forward and putting their weight on their knuckles, which blocked the flow of blood. On the other hand, if they had their weight back on their heels, their knuckles would be red. They would be in reactive mode, not being aggressive.

In real life, we were lined up for a punt, I saw the red knuckles and I knew the guys weren't going to charge. That meant there was a chance I could make a play. Right there, I called the audible "Check Zero" to the other guys on special teams. Everybody slid right so that there was one position in the line left open. I took a step to the right, ran underneath, and I was gone. I heard the guys on the other side say, "Oh shit."

The stadium went silent. Our punter, Mike Michelle, nailed one right outside of the end zone. I got there before anyone else and laid a savage hit on the opposing punt returner. He fumbled and I scooped up the ball and ran into the end zone thinking I had my first NFL touchdown. Unfortunately, the officials called it a "muff" and placed the ball on the seven-yard line. On the next play we scored and we won the game. After the game I got invited to my first team party. I was really an Eagle. That is what I mean when I say analyze, adapt and achieve.

## STILL ACHIEVING

JANET: I wasn't given anything. Adapting has been my whole life. Am I tough? Yes. Am I a taskmaster? Yes. But I've had to be. I still want to achieve. I still want to be great at something else. I play golf and now I have a goal: I want to be my club champion. I want to be good at whatever I try. If I don't get there, it's okay. I've learned to enjoy the experience.

I want to keep myself in shape and age gracefully. I want to

> **INVINCIBLE WISDOM**
>
> *Analyze your life in terms of its environment. Are the things around you helping you toward success - or are they holding you back*
>
> — *W. Clement Stone*

give back and impact other people. I was an athlete, and then suddenly that applause was gone. I moved on. I became a teacher and a coach and I was able to pull things out of kids that no one else could. I helped them experience life and laugh at it. Then I adapted again. I became an entrepreneur and a businesswoman.

Vince and I have both adapted in life many times, because that's what life is. It's one long adaptation. That's what we do as human beings. I don't ever want to stop adapting and stop achieving new things. I trained to get 10s in gymnastics; I don't know how to be a 7.5. Anybody can do this. You keep your eyes open, be willing to jump at the next thing that comes along, and give it everything you have. It's not a complicated formula, but it takes heart, determination and belief.

## LEARN TO READ THE MOMENT

**VINCE:** As we come to the close of our time together, I hope I've given you a lot of tools and ideas to help you win during changing, challenging times. With everything else I've talked about, the concept of analyze, adapt, achieve is the perfect wrap-up. I based my NFL career on this advice and I've based my life since football on it too. Here's what it means, broken down:

- **Analyze:** Read what's going on around you in real time. Understand the significance of it—the people, the relationships, the power plays. Educate yourself so you know what's really happening.

- **Adapt:** Respond quickly to events and be prepared to change your plans on a dime. Notice that I didn't say "react" quickly? That's because a reaction is pure reflex; there's no thought to it.  Responding means you have information and you're making a conscious choice on how to act.

- **Achieve:** Seize the advantage that a quick change of strategy can give you and run with the ball!  See it through to the end, put in the work, and don't stop until you've reached your goal.

Basically, if you're not reading the moment and adapting, you're wasting your time.  These days, change happens at the speed of the Internet.  The pace of business is faster, information goes around the world in the blink of an eye, and if you can't make split-second decisions to go after an opportunity or trust a new contact, you're going to be left behind.  You need to become a student of the world you live in—the whole world, really. You should know as much as you can about your goals.  Study, learn and change.

For me in that punt play, analyze came when I read the defender's knuckles and knew he would be back on his heels.  Adapt was when I called that audible.  Achieve came when I made the hit and we got the win.  In a business meeting, you might analyze beforehand by learning everything you can about the people, the company, the product and the market.  You'd adapt by changing your tactics on the fly when the client throws you a curve.  You would achieve by creating a whole new opportunity for your company through your quick and creative thinking.

## THE SNAP DECISION COMES FROM PREPARATION

Remember when we talked about the fundamentals and I said that the sports plays that looked spontaneous and easy were really the product of endless hard work and repetition?  The same is true in business, law, science, teaching or any other occupation.  The only way you gain the knowledge and savvy to make snap judgments that turn out to be right is by becoming a scholar of your field.

Preparation is everything.  Ballplayers watch game videos and run drills.  Attorneys study precedents and depose witnesses.  Parents pack activities for their kids on long car trips and have lists of all the attractions along the route. Brilliant surprises are never accidental. They're the visible end point of a long process of study, digging, asking questions and refining ideas.

Remember when SEAL Team Six took out Osama bin Laden? Of course you do; it was one of the most emotional events any of us has lived through since 9/11. We've all memorized the details: the daring flight into Pakistan, the malfunctioning helicopter that had to be blown up, the raid on the compound and the final extermination of one of the world's most wanted criminals. It was a great day to be an American.

But it was also an example of analyze, adapt and achieve. President Obama and his national security team had multiple options in taking out bin Laden, and the first was dropping bombs remotely. It would have not risked American lives, but there might have been collateral damage and we would never have known if we'd gotten our man. But the president had an ace up his sleeve: years of intelligence gathered about every part of the compound and everyone thought to be in it. That was the analysis. The adaptation came when the commanders decided to send in the SEAL team instead. The achievement was a near-perfect military operation that got its objective and didn't lose a single American. But it would not have been possible without incredible study and preparation.

## INVINCIBLE MOMENT

*Theresa Sareo shares her Invincible Moment:*

*"I woke up struggling out of an induced coma at Bellevue Hospital in Manhattan on Father's Day, 2002. I had no idea how I got there or what was wrong but I knew from a very deep place that I was in major trouble. What lay ahead of me was a devastation I could never have imagined or seen coming.*

*"I couldn't yet open my eyes fully when I heard my mother's voice say: 'Theresa, it's Mom, you were in a bad accident and are in the hospital, but you're going to be okay.' I didn't believe her and started shaking my head 'No.' I knew that I was definitely NOT okay.*

*"I was told a few days later what happened. I was standing on*

the corner of 34th and Park Ave. waiting to cross the street when an impaired driver of an SUV made an illegal turn. He ended up crashing into me, pinning me against a three-foot high metal post which severed my right leg at my hip joint on impact. My femoral artery was bleeding out over half of my blood onto the street. Thanks to the love of total strangers who somehow held my broken body together until EMS arrived, I survived this horrific, unbelievable nightmare.

"Looking back over the past nine years, I can reflect on this journey in awe and explain that survival, for me, came in two parts. Initially, people who love and care about you have to hold you up until you can hold yourself up. This is not an easy choice for them and it takes the collective commitment of a village—which, in my case, included a combination of medical caregivers, family, friends and strangers. Each one played a vital role and if one had been out of place, my successful recovery would have taken much longer. I was so blessed to have had the complete package, which is why I now dedicate my life and music career in service to others who may not be as fortunate. That subsequently led me to working with our wounded military, who represent the ultimate example of giving service.

"Nothing provides more personal perspective or gratification than spreading genuine brotherly love. This basic rule of life becomes crystal clear in receiving it when you need it most. For me, that powerful healing exchange started when I was a hospital patient visiting and singing for other trauma patients, which has since become a career of speaking and singing engagements around the world.

"When it comes to facing adversity, bilateral lower limb amputee Mark Little of the Paralyzed Veteran's Association said it best: 'We're fortunate our eyes have been opened, so we can take every day and really make the best of it.' That journey from grief to gratitude is long and can seem like an endless test of courage. But if you can somehow choose love, and say yes through it all, you will find what can be all the joy you deserve in living your very own, truly invincible life."

## TRUST YOURSELF UNDER PRESSURE

What about adapting? All that information might make instant decisions seem easier, but they're not. It takes a lot of guts to make quick calls under pressure. Just ask a surgeon whose patient has died on the table and who has five minutes to get his heart restarted. When the chips are down and you've got to improvise, there's one thing you have to have: trust in your ability to make good decisions when the pressure is on.

That takes practice. I've found that the best executives are the ones who have learned to rely on their instincts instead of questioning and second-guessing themselves. The same is true for top coaches, doctors, you name it. In some fields, like law enforcement and the military, you've got no choice: if you don't make the right call in that split-second, people die. So you learn to believe in your ability to improvise and to make sound decisions in the blink of an eye. That's what it means to adapt.

### JANET'S WORDS FOR WOMEN

*Don't try to be something you're not. Be great at what you can be great at, even if other people don't understand it. If everyone was great at the same thing, we'd all be pretty boring. Women tend to be pretty intuitive, but you need to work on the analytical part of your brain. Dream but also be critical in your thinking. See what the opportunity is, but don't ignore the pitfalls.*

One of the best examples of this that I've ever seen came at the Atlanta 500, which my family and I were lucky enough to attend in 2011, sitting in pit seats, no less. The Red Bull Racing Team #83 car, under the leadership of my pal Jay Frye, blew me away with their execution of analyze, adapt and achieve under immense pressure. Brian Vickers was in the chase for the win that day, and because he has bonuses in his contract for a high finish in the major marquee races, there was a ton at stake. He was in the top ten and running great when he made a routine pit stop.

Well, Brian's pit was right next to Jimmy Johnson's pit, and the Johnson pit crew "inadvertently" let a tire roll out in front of Brian's car just as he was pulling out to rejoin the race. Brian hit the brakes and BAM! His rear axle snapped. Race over, right? Not even close. He had a yellow caution flag, so he had time. He was able to

> ## INVINCIBLE WISDOM
>
> *"If you're trying to achieve, there will be roadblocks. I've had them; everybody has had them. But obstacles don't have to stop you. If you run into a wall, don't turn around and give up. Figure out how to climb it, go through it, or work around it."*
>
> — Michael Jordan

nurse the car around the caution lap, and during that time, his incredible crew managed to get another axle from a crew 80 yards away, get it to the pit and have a team of guys ready to pull Brian in and get that new axle on in a matter of seconds. Thanks to their speedy action and the caution flag, they actually got him back in the race and kept him in the top ten.

One of the crew guys even had to go over the track wall to get the axle, and my son Vinny gave him the mandatory helmet that he needed to do that. It was quite a display of grace under pressure. They saw the problem, found a solution and got it done.

## KNOW HOW TO SEAL THE DEAL

Finally, there's achieving. In the context of analyze and adapt, this isn't the kind of long-term achievement that we talk about in college graduation speeches. It's situational. It's about seeing the problem, breaking it down in a split second, doing your best McGyver impression to find a fix, and making something great happen in the moment. That's what I mean by "seal the deal."

Sealing the deal means having the underlying skills to make your adaptive solution work. For instance, on that punt play I talked about to start this chapter, the only reason I was able to make my audible work was that I had the skills to come off the line fast, run the right route to the kick returner, and execute a proper hit on him. If I fail at any one of those things, we lose. So achieve could also be called execute: pulling together all your skill, talent and knowledge in the moment of need and getting it done.

How do you do that? Practice, working on the fundamentals, being disciplined—so many of the things we've already talked about in this book. You work to develop excellence in all the key areas of your field, so that when the time comes and the pressure is on, you can perform and deliver. The only way that happens is through endless hard work. Even the superstars do it; that's how they remain superstars. Years ago, there was a magazine story about basketball legend Larry Bird and how he had finally started lifting weights in the off-season. Bird had become the NBA's best player despite not being able to run or jump a lick, but now here he was, at the peak of his career, sweating it out in the gym and coming to camp suddenly dunking down to his elbows. One opposing player said, "That's all we need, a Larry Bird who can run and jump."

Bird didn't have to practice and work like that. Neither did Michael Jordan or Magic Johnson. Neither do Madonna, Lady Gaga, or Neil Diamond. They train so hard and make it look so easy. Navy SEALs are already incredibly fit and well trained, so why do they continually drill and practice and work out? Because you never know when you're going to be called to take out the world's worst terrorist.

That's the basis of your greatness. Try to make the most of everything else I've shared about being invincible and realizing your potential, but if you do one thing, do this: never stop trying to get better. Take what you're already good at and find ways to continually improve even more. Become the best, even if no one else realizes it. If frustrated go back to the basics. Shore up your weak spots as best you can, but really zero in on your talents and strengths, because when the pressure is on, that's what will make you a difference maker for your team.

## END ZONE

**Things to think about & do after finishing this chapter**

■ Review all the previous End Zone material in this book.

■ Write down the things you need to learn so that you can better analyze what's happening in your profession or occupation.

_____

_____

_____

_____

_____

■ Think about how you can trust your own improvisation and adaptation skills. How can you put yourself in position to have to make snap judgments so you learn to trust yourself?

_____

_____

_____

_____

_____

■ Write down the skills that you're already good at but that you can improve upon.

_____

_____

_____

_____

_____

## Let's recap all the lessons in invincibility that we've talked about together:

- See your vision for the future and know its cost.

- Make your plan.

- Know your Invincible Moment.

- Master the fundamentals.

- Know what you're fighting for.

- Work harder than you've ever worked before.

- Find a great mentor.

- Be ready to reinvent yourself.

- Know the role you should be playing.

- Bring your passion to what you do.

- Take care of your body.

- Go the extra degree.

- Find what you're good at and work on being great at it.

- Think positive.

- Reward yourself for the small victories.

- Build a team of people who respect and support you.

- Avoid people who will tear you down.

- Stop fearing failure.

- Analyze, adapt and achieve.

# NOW LET'S GET STARTED!

1) **What invincible moment inspired you?**

_____

_____

_____

2) **Why?** _____

_____

3) **Who are the people who support and believe in you?**

_____

_____

_____

4) **What is your goal?** _____

_____

5) **What changes do you have to make to realize your goal?**

_____

_____

_____

6) **What is your game plan to reach that goal ?**

_____

_____

_____

7) **What will be your reward when your goal is a reality?**

_____

_____

_____

# CHAPTER TWENTY

# INVINCIBLE
# CORPORATIONS

*Ridiculous yachts and private planes and
big limousines won't make people enjoy life
more…it's about getting a balance.*

— Richard Branson

When I speak in front of 10,000 people at a huge corporate retreat for companies like Best Buy, MetLife, Disney, Bristol-Meyers Squibb, Heinz and others (for a full list, go to my website at www.vincepapale.com), one of the questions that always comes up is, "How can you make what you're saying relevant for my company and my people?" Well, that's an easy one. The tools and principles of invincibility are relevant to every person at virtually every company.

We're in a period of unforeseen economic turmoil, but even when times are good, life in Corporate America is challenging. Workers are always being asked to do more, be more, and be on call more. You're often expected to check email on vacation, work weekends and sacrifice your personal life for the good of the company. But is that really benefiting the company, and is it really benefiting you? I'd suggest that it's not. More than ever, employees, managers and executives need to know how to juggle hard work and restorative play, deal with stress in a healthy way, protect their body and mind and work smarter to increase their own productivity. That's something that Janet and I will be doing as part of a new program: Invincible Corporations corporate training.

## SOLUTIONS FOR PERSONAL GROWTH

**JANET:** Vince and I feel that the pieces of advice in this book can apply to anyone at just about any stage of life and place in his or her career, from young college graduates only in the workforce for a few years to senior executives. The wisdom that we talk about—work hard, have passion, make a plan, think positive—has been around for a long time. But I don't think anyone has boiled it down to something this simple and accessible. Basically, we're here to teach people in the organizational environment how to be more resilient, hopeful and self-aware human beings. That will make them better employees, managers and leaders.

The corporate world is so demanding and fast-paced that it's easy for people to simply react to the demands they face. There's no plan. You put in the hours, try to have a personal life, try to get ahead as best you can, and hope things work out. Well, hope is not a success strategy. That approach is the reason that so many employees are stressed out, turnover is high, absenteeism is rampant, and "presenteeism," where peo-

> INVINCIBLE WISDOM

> INVINCIBLE WISDOM

*"The big secret in life is that there is no big secret. Whatever your goal, you can get there if you're willing to work."*

— *Oprah Winfrey*

ple are at work but not fully present, is increasing. Our goal is to help motivate personnel individually and in groups, encourage employees to think in new ways and to develop complete toolkits for dealing with the demands of professional and personal life…and coming out winners.

## INVINCIBILITY TRAINING

**VINCE:** We're not going to claim that the lessons that produce success on a football field are going to have the same effect on a company's market share or stock price. That's pretty simplistic. Business is not sports, and it's not war. However, the principles of invincibility are universal. They're about more than football. They are a recipe for a more fulfilling, prosperous, resilient life—and that includes your life within a large corporation, non-profit or governmental organization.

In these settings, people constantly face the same kinds of questions Janet and I have during our athletic and business careers. How do I motivate myself? How do I ignore the doubters? How do I get an edge on the competition? How do I take better care of my body and my mind? How you answer those questions has a lot to do with how you'll handle the demands of your job, cope with stress, advance in your career and balance work, health and relationships. People who have success in those areas become better employees, in the long term making their companies more successful.

When we come into your company with our Invincible Corporations program, these are some of the solutions we offer:

1. **Work-Life Balance:** We work with your people to help them figure out the areas of their family and personal lives that are suffering and change their priorities.

2. **Stress Management:** Stress damages physical and mental health more than just about any other cause. We train individuals in the many means of managing stress and reducing its dangerous effects.

3. **Character and Ethics:** How do you chase success and still keep your character and ethical center? It is possible. We'll talk about how.

4. **Corporate Health and Wellness:** The company grind can take a toll on weight, blood pressure, mental health and more. We present efficient strategies for exercise, diet, supplementation and more.

5. **Team Building and Leadership:** Leadership isn't about position, but action. I didn't become Special Teams captain of the Eagles because I was the most experienced player, but because I embodied what the team was supposed to be about. We teach managers and executives how to bring out their true strengths.

6. **Failing Forward:** Too often, companies punish bold risk taking because sometimes, risk becomes failure. But failure leads to discovery and ultimate success. However, instead of the societal norm of focusing on one's weaknesses we will shift the focus to understanding and leveraging one's strengths! We help learners reframe failure and find ways to reward smart risk.

7. **Crisis Management:** Invincibility is all about taking the worst the world has to offer, staying upright and fighting back successfully. We present mental and business strategies for facing economic downturns, personnel problems and other disasters and coming out on top.

8. **Creativity and Reinvention:** Encourage your people to recreate their own positions and think outside the cubicle to help your company be more competitive. We share tactics for reinventing yourself and your organization.

9. **Understand Thyself:** It's simply knowing your strengths, leveraging them and preparing your team for the opportunities for which each member is best suited.

## HOW WE TRAIN

**JANET:** But it's not just about what we do. It's how we do it and who we are. Vince and I are both survivors, people who have overcome long odds and many people's doubts to do things that others only dream about. We're resilient and we know how to improvise. Most importantly, we've got a strong sense of who we are and what we can do—something that can be hard to maintain when you're in a corporate environment where you're told that the individual doesn't matter.

You DO matter. You have the power not only to improve your own life but the position of your company. The two are closely related. That's why we approach corporate training from a personal angle, with humor, honesty, and plainspoken wisdom, not flip charts and step-by-step processes. Some of the ways in which we deliver our lessons:

- Motivational speaking for small groups all the way up to meetings of hundreds or conferences of thousands.

- Workshops—Half-day, all-day, or weekend.

- Breakout sessions for small or large groups, featuring more intensive discussion, exercises and interaction.

- Team building training camps, structured like football training camps and intended to encourage teamwork and trust.

- Individual coaching—One-to-one work in private sessions addressing a full range of invincibility questions.

## OUR GOALS

**VINCE:** As anyone who has seen me speak knows, I'm all about positive thinking and self-belief. At the beginning of this book, Janet and I wrote that everything begins with belief. If you don't believe you can do something, all the methods and plans in the world don't mean anything. But there's only so much that I can teach by example. It's tough for me to tell somebody to just be like Vince Papale when

# INVINCIBLE MOMENT

*Olympic gold medal swimmer Theresa Andrews shares her Invincible Moment:*

"Back in 1983, when I was going for the Olympics in 1984, I had the title of "almost there" swimmer hanging over my head. I had missed in 1980 by .3 seconds. At the Pan American Games, I'd missed coming in third by a couple hundredths of a second. So coming into 1984, I had very little support.

"I was planning to come back to Baltimore to train, because I knew that at home, I would get support from family. I have 11 brothers and sisters. I was just hoping to make the team. Not long after that, my brother Danny, a lacrosse player for the University of North Carolina, was riding his bike when he was struck by a car and paralyzed from the waist down. I came home from the University of Florida to help care for him as he learned to live in a wheelchair.

"In all my life, after training for about 15 years, I had never wanted to quit swimming until that point. I quit that year. I felt like a failure, and I didn't want to fail anymore. I went to Danny's hospital where he was doing his rehab, and told him that I was going to quit. He said, 'No, you have to go back. We haven't finished our goal.'

"It turned out that every day, I was his last visitor. We would talk about our days, and over those months he was secretly formulating a goal for us as a team. I said, 'How can you compare athletics and rehabilitation? What I'm doing is nothing.'

"He replied, 'My goal is not about me, whether I walk again or not. Your goal isn't making the team or not making it. Our goal this year is not to allow people to impose limitations on us.' That was a life-changing moment. I was holding myself back. I was my worst opponent. At that moment, my brother set me free.

"I went back that December and trained, made the team and won gold medals in the 100-meter backstroke and the 400-meter medley relay. I gave the one for the backstroke to Danny. He went on to law school, was a prosecutor for ten years, and is now a judge with three kids. He only knows how to go 100 miles an hour, even in a wheelchair."

they're struggling with career burnout or trying to balance a demanding job with a family crisis.

So in Invincible Corporations programs, we aim to do much more. Through storytelling, practical examples, asking hard questions, exercises, writing assignments, cooperative tasks and other methods, our goals are to change how you think, act and react in the following ways:

- **Be more self-aware.** When you're able to step back and recognize your own thought patterns and habits, you can change the ones that aren't working.

- **Stop fearing failure.** Risk is an element of everyone's success strategy; it makes no sense to fear it. You'll learn how to make risk your friend and stop judging yourself by your failures.

- **Trust your strength.** Plenty of people have no idea how much endurance they have until the chips are down. We'll teach you to recognize the signs of strength in yourself.

- **Take back your time.** It's in every company's best interest to have people who are well balanced, happy and healthy. Time management and mental tools help you discover what's most important to you and find the time to enjoy it.

- **Be healthier.** We'll talk about proven research into exercise, diet, supplementation and rest and help you develop a plan for improving your health over the long term.

- **Stop being stressed out.** The stress response is a killer. But there are many ways to keep deadlines, pressure and other people's drama from turning you into a stroke patient.

The benefits of invincibility training to companies are many: better morale, improved productivity, less absenteeism, more engaged workers, lower turnover, better retention of information and improved customer care from people who are happier with their jobs and themselves. There's nobody who doesn't win.

## INVINCIBLE WORKERS?

**JANET:** Whether we work with a few key managers in a company or the entire staff of a corporation in multiple locations, the impact is the same. Healthy individuals equal thriving companies.

We're going through a time when everyone is working longer hours for the same pay, facing "speeded up" workloads and worrying about job security. It's a time of great anxiety for everyone from the receptionist all the way up to the C-suite. Wouldn't your organization benefit from people who knew how to work hard, go the extra degree, find their passion in their work, deal with stress productively, build effective teams and inspire others?

**VINCE:** Those are some of the things that Invincible Corporations training can offer. Janet and I have lived the lessons and survived to become happier, healthier and more prosperous than ever before, all while raising healthy kids and being contributing members of our community. It is possible to do all that and more…IF you know how to go about it.

---

Find out more about our Invincible Corporations training programs for companies of all sizes at www.vincepapale.com. And watch for our upcoming books in the "Invincible" series:

- **Invincible Kids:** Giving Children the Tools for a Successful Life in an Age of Entitlement

- **Invincible Moments: Getting the Last Laugh.** Incredible Stories of Personal Courage and Strength

- **Invincible Marriage:** Twenty Secrets for Growing Together and Staying Together

- **Invincible Boomers:** Eating Well, Moving Well and Living Well at 65 and Far Beyond

# TWO-MINUTE DRILL

Let's take one final moment, or two, to re-cap what you've just read here? What's your plan? Who's trying to pull you down? What are you up against? What are you going to do about it? What is your Invincible Moment? Did you take the time to define your strengths and make them stronger?

In every obstacle we face, individually, or as a team we really do go thru the simple mental exercise called:
**ANALYZE, ADAPT & ACHIEVE.**

- Do as much research on the challenge at hand. Get as much information as you can and try to be logical rather than emotional about your approach. Know your opponent. POGO once said "we just met the enemy and he is us." How true sometimes. A bad attitude is your worst adversary.

- Get those game plans ready, and we do mean plans. Rarely do things go as smoothly as you'd like. Have your audible (Plan B) ready for when the time comes to use it. Improvise and adjust and be on the balls of your feet. If you need to go back to the fundamentals. When in doubt go back to the basics.

- Get it done. Make it happen. You know you can do it. And if you fall short, so what … just never quit. Go that extra degree. Be the best you can be, surround yourself with good people, and take care of your own business.

*There's that greatness, potential, in you that's just waiting to burst out. It's never too late to get into the game. **BE INVINCIBLE!***

## ACKNOWLEDGEMENTS

*Janet and I are forever indebted to the many teachers, coaches and mentors who impacted our life and guided us while we chased our dreams ...*

Bill & Ginny Coco          Kevin Quinn
Vannie Edwards             Dr. Jack Ramsey
George Corner              Fred Turoff
Abie Grossfeld             Marty Stern
Muriel Grossfeld           Dick Vermeil
Lou Nicastro

*You are nothing without family who believe in you and love you. Thank you ...*

Janet Cantwell & Gerry Cantwell
Frank & Almira Papale
Janet's Brothers & Sisters: Diane, Susan, Geralyn, Patty, Barbara, Gerard, Kenny and Tina
Vince's Sister Janice & Nephews Brad & Kirk
Both of our many Aunts, Uncles and Cousins

*To Gabriella & Vincent, our amazing children, whose dreams we share with them. We love you unconditionally.*

*To our Invincible Team that helped make this book happen ...*

Tim Vandehey               Frank Assumma
Rob DeVitis                Bruce Casella
Dave Van Dusen             Rose Cunningham
Russ Brown                 Jodi Ritzen
Stacey Granger             Patrice Cohill
Jerry Manas                Nancy Ottaviano

*A huge thank you to the amazing men and women who shared with us their Invincible Moments and touched our hearts showing all of us what courage and perseverance is all about. And also thank you to those who took the time to share with you on the back cover their thoughts about us.*

*continued on next page*

*Acknowledgements continued from previous page*

**We would also like to thank our incredible Teammates at Market America for their extraordinary supplements we have been taking for the past 15 years and for making the new Invincible Health and Wellness Isotonix a reality. This book has gotten their unwavering support from the very beginning. Our thanks to ...**

JR & Loren Ridinger
Marty Weissman
Dennis Franks
Science and Product Development Teams

---

**As you know we do our best to eat healthy and we really appreciate Ray Rastelli and The Rastelli Food Group for their natural, organic and steroid free meats that our entire family eats.**

---

**Our fitness mentor is a Certified Athletic Trainer that we met on the set of Invincible 6 years ago. Today he is our family fitness mentor guiding us to stay trim, fit and happy. Thanks to our buddy Brian Nguyen.**

---

**We are celebrating the 5th Anniversary of the release of the movie Invincible and if it weren't for the movie there probably wouldn't have been this book. With that in mind I can't thank the following people enough ...**

Ken Mok
Walt Disney Productions
Mark Ciardi & Gordon Gray at Mayhem
Victor Constantino
Mark Wahlberg, Greg Kinnear, Elizabeth Banks & Michael Nouri
The All Star Invincible Cast

---

**A Special Thanks to the Premier Crozer-Keystone Orthopaedics Partnership**

216

# YOU CAN BE INVINCIBLE

We've created a new website so you can share your Invincible Moment. Perhaps your Last Laugh will be part of our Be Invincible Series. We are also looking for stories about "Invincible Kidz"—kids who have done inspiring, incredible things. For more details please visit:

www.YouCanBeInvincible.com

---

As you know, the only way to reach your full potential is to live a healthy lifestyle. For the past 15 years we have made some amazing isotonic supplements part of our daily vitamin and fitness routine. For more information on those supplements, and our exiting new Isotonix Prime Invincible Health & Wellness Formula, simply go to:

www.isotonix.com

---

Prime Invincible was developed by our friends at Market America. For more information on all of their supplements, products and services check out:

www.marketamerica.com

---

*Life is all about the choices you make, surrounding yourself with a character team and implementing your plan. Remember, happy are those who dream dreams and are willing to pay the price to make their dreams come true. Are you willing to pay the price?*